Guide to the Perplexing
A SURVIVAL MANUAL
for Women in Religious Studies

First Edition

THE AMERICAN ACADEMY OF RELIGION
INDIVIDUAL VOLUMES

Individual Volumes, No. 2
Guide to the Perplexing
A SURVIVAL MANUAL
for Women in Religious Studies

First Edition

By Members of the Committee
on the Status of Women in the Profession
of the American Academy of Religion

Guide to the Perplexing
A SURVIVAL MANUAL
for Women in Religious Studies

First Edition

*By Members of the Committee
on the Status of Women in the Profession
of the American Academy of Religion*

Scholars Press
Atlanta, Georgia

THE AMERICAN ACADEMY OF RELIGION
INDIVIDUAL VOLUMES

Guide to the Perplexing
A SURVIVAL MANUAL
for Women in Religious Studies

First Edition

© 1992
The American Academy of Religion

Library of Congress Cataloging-in-Publication Data
Guide to the perplexing: a survival manual for women in religious
  studies/ by members of the Committee on the Status of Women in the
  Profession of the American Academy of Religion.
      p. cm. — (American Academy of Religion individual volumes;
  no. 2)
      ISBN 1-55540-803-6 (pbk.)
      1. Religion—Study and teaching—Vocational guidance. 2. Women
  Biblical scholars—Vocational guidance.   I. American Academy of
  Religion. Committee on the Status of Women in the Profession.
  II. Series.
  BL41.G843 1992
  200'.71—dc20   92-38548
                                                          CIP

Printed in the United States of America
on acid-free paper

INTRODUCTION

For those of us who remember when women members of the AAR/SBL could be counted on the fingers of very few hands, the increasing number of women in the field of religion is an exciting and welcome development. The rise in numbers of women, however, has not always meant an easy time for women starting out in the field; nor has it meant that women no longer face isolation. Individual women still find themselves pioneers in particular departments, or, if they have fellow graduate students and junior faculty as colleagues, they still know few senior women who can function as friends and mentors. Moreover, in some ways, the larger number of women in the AAR/SBL militates against the easy exchange of information that characterized a more embattled era, so that much of the oral tradition concerning the trials and victories of women in religious studies is not being passed on.

It is for these reasons that the American Academy of Religion Committee on the Status of Women in the Profession (AARCSWP) decided to write a Survival Manual to help and encourage new women scholars. Most of the material for this manual is gleaned either from personal experience or the rich oral tradition shared by many women of the AAR/SBL. The authors have relied on their own wisdom, on the wisdom of colleagues who provided feedback on drafts, on conversations with women scholars in religion and the AAR/SBL Women's Caucus: Religious Studies and on the survival manuals of the American Historical Association and the Modern Language Association. The opinions expressed are our own and do not necessarily represent the opinions or advice of the American Academy of Religion, its board of directors or staff.

We hope that the information presented here will be helpful to new scholars in the field attempting to negotiate the mine-field of an academic career. In telling war stories or cautioning new faculty members about the pitfalls of certain choices, it is not our intent to frighten people or to suggest that everyone will meet discrimination or even problems. Rather, we want to enable women to be pro-active, to have the knowledge that will enable them to avoid certain common dangers, and to meet other dangers without the feelings of personal failure or self-blame that so often are born of isolation. While the manual is written explicitly for women, much of it should be helpful to men starting out in their careers, as well as to departments hiring women.

No manual can substitute for personal conversation and sharing or joint action on the issues that confront women in the Academy. These are the purposes of the Women's Caucus: Religious Studies and we encourage every woman who finds this manual useful to join. The Caucus has, for a number of years, conducted an excellent workshop on professional development for women entering the field of religion. This manual and the workshop--which takes place the day before the AAR/SBL annual meeting each year--together should provide women in the field a strong set of resources for starting to build a successful career.

Since we anticipate that this manual will be reprinted, we very much hope readers will share with us their responses and concerns. What advice is particularly helpful or unhelpful? What topics are missing that ought to be included? Are there ideas or personal experiences you would like to share with others in the next edition? Letters can be sent to the AARCSWP through the AAR executive office, 1703 Clifton Rd. NE, Suite G5, Atlanta, GA 30329-4019.

A final cautionary note: the information in this document is not intended to substitute for professional legal advice. If a situation arises, either in an interview or employment setting, which requires legal action, the best thing to do is to consult an attorney, immediately (there are sometimes short time limits for filing complaints). The American Association of University Professors, the National Organization for Women, and the American Civil Liberties Union can all help you find lawyers who specialize in sex and/or race discrimination cases. The Lambda Legal Defense Fund can provide information on lawyers specializing in discrimination based on sexual orientation. The AAUP also provides advice for faculty contemplating legal action.

The chapters on the job search, interviewing, negotiating an offer, and professional development were drafted by Rita Nakashima Brock of Hamline University, with feedback and suggestions from Veena Deo and Andrea Bell of Hamline University, Susan Brooks Thistlethwaite of Chicago Theological Seminary, Patricia Killen of Pacific Lutheran University, and members of the Committee on the Status of Women in the Profession. In addition, she consulted Becoming a Historian: A Survival

<u>Manual</u> <u>for</u> <u>Women</u> <u>and</u> <u>Men</u>, by Melanie Gustafson (Washington D.C.: American Historical Association, 1991) and <u>A</u> <u>Career</u> <u>Guide</u> <u>for</u> <u>Ph.</u> <u>D.s</u> <u>and</u> <u>Ph.</u> <u>D.</u> <u>Candidates</u> <u>in</u> <u>English</u> <u>and</u> <u>Foreign</u> <u>Languages</u>, by Elaine Showalter (New York: The Modern Language Association of America, 1985). Judith Plaskow of Manhattan College drafted the chapters on first year faculty and promotion and tenure, with feedback and suggestions from Julie Leininger Pycior of Manhattan College, Emily Erwin Culpepper of the University of the Redlands, and members of the CSWP. She also consulted <u>Becoming</u> <u>a</u> <u>Historian</u>. Kelly Brown Douglas wrote material on the special concerns of women of color and interspersed it in a number of chapters, and Judith Plaskow did the same for lesbian issues. The maternity and childcare chapter was composed by Paula Fredriksen of Boston University, A. J. Levine of Swarthmore College, and Susan Thistlethwaite. Finally, the chapter on sexual harassment was written by James Poling of Colgate Rochester Divinity School, Adele McCollum, Montclair State College, and Rita N. Brock. The section on amorous relationships was written by Rita N. Brock, and Susan Thistlethwaite, as committee chair, offered the conclusion.

We look forward to increasing numbers of women in the field of religious studies and hope this manual contributes to greater success for our newer colleagues. Survival is important, but the satisfaction of thriving in a career is something we want to encourage for all who find this manual helpful.

Rita Nakashima Brock and Judith Plaskow
For the Committee on the Status of Women in the Profession

Members of the AARCSWP:
Rita Nakashima Brock, Kelly Brown Douglas, Paula Fredriksen, Adele McCollum, Judith Plaskow, James Poling, and Susan Thistlethwaite

*To the Women
in Religious Studies
who have gone
before us*

CHAPTER ONE: THE JOB SEARCH

Aside from the AAR Openings, women looking for academic appointments should check The Women's Review of Books, The Chronicle of Higher Education, and the NWSA Newsletter, all of which advertise jobs. In addition, the newsletter of the Women's Caucus: Religious Studies publishes notices of job openings sent to them by members. Membership in the Women's Caucus provides a subscription to the newsletter, as well as other benefits, such as information about the workshops for women starting out in the profession which the Caucus offers just before the AAR annual meeting. In addition, membership in the Caucus provides a support system for women in the academy.

As you search for openings, think carefully about the kind of position that best suits your skills and interests. You needn't have a specific job in mind to think through the kinds of features you want in an institution and position that would use your training and abilities well. It helps to arrive at some clarity about your career goals and objectives and to locate the positions that best suit you. In considering your goals, think about the kind of institution that will fit your career objectives: for example, you may best be suited to a seminary if your religious involvements are important to you, or to a small teaching-oriented college if heavy demands to publish do not interest you. Consider also parts of the country to which you are willing to move. Unless you are absolutely desperate for any job at all, you should avoid a scattershot approach to jobs.

1

2

I.   The Cover Letter

The cover letter first presents you to a search committee. Take care to make sure it is well done and carefully considered. Do not write and mail generic application letters. Keep in mind that a generic-sounding cover letter may carry a subliminal message that you are either not especially interested in the position or you are desperate (which will make the committee wonder why no one else has hired you). Tailor each letter to the advertised position. Keep a detailed description of the position in mind as you write this letter and let that description guide the content of the letter. Explain how you fit the position's requirements and discuss what you can offer. It is also appropriate to add things you would offer beyond the requirements for the position.

Avoid skewing yourself toward a job for which you are not really qualified. Search committees generally see through such things quickly and will weed you out. Misrepresenting yourself for a position may imply an unacceptable level of dishonesty to a search committee. Search committees are potential colleagues and should be treated forthrightly and respectfully. If you do not exactly fit the job description and are applying anyway, explain why. For example, one of us got two jobs without fitting either description, but explained that, while in a different field, she could teach all the required courses associated with the position.

Do not use the cover letter to repeat information in your *vita* or in your placement file. Search committees reviewing numerous dossiers will not take kindly to rereading information. If you want to call attention to something in your *vita*, do so in the context of a further discussion of that angle of your work. For example, if you list a current position without much description, spell out your accomplishments in more detail. The cover letter should update any further work you are doing beyond the published work listed on your *vita*, including any discussions you are having with publishers. You might also mention forthcoming publications, major papers at conferences, etc.

It doesn't hurt, either, to state your interest in the institution, if you are familiar with it or with someone already on the faculty. If time permits, research the particular kind of institution involved and its needs. Seminaries, church-related universities, state institutions, graduate schools, women's colleges, African American or Native American colleges, teaching-oriented or research-oriented institutions--all have their own personalities. If you know something in particular about the institution involved, address what you know in the cover letter by describing what you would offer such an institution. Or if you know the work of some of the faculty, you might comment on their contributions to the field.

Additional information to include in your letter are such things as international travel experience, work outside the field that affects your thinking about religion, or some special research opportunity that meant a lot to you--these help you look distinctive. Also if you have travel plans that affect your availability for interviews, let the committee know when you will be available and how best to reach you. Be careful about this however. If you plan to be abroad and are afraid this will affect your candidacy, let them know when you will be in the country. Do not pressure them to give you an early interview date or suggest they bend their rules. This can look manipulative. It is up to the search committee to decide how they will handle complications. If they feel you are one of the best candidates for the job, they will find a way to interview you.

A letter of up to two pages--no more--is reasonable. One page, concisely written, is better. Include a paragraph about your interest in this particular position, one about your scholarly work, and one about your current employment (if it is similar to the job you seek). For search committees, which often read anywhere from 20 to 200 dossiers, concise letters are a godsend. If your letter is too long, it may not get enough attention. On the other hand, don't sell yourself short by not saying enough.

If an institution asks you to submit a personal statement with your application, stay within the limits of the assignment. If there is no stated limit, call and ask. The last thing search committees want is extra work.

II. Reference Letters

If a list of references is requested, be sure all those you list have already agreed to serve and be sure they can be contacted by the committee. For example, if one of your references will be out of the country on sabbatical, it might be wise to select someone else.

You should consider carefully whom to ask for letters of reference. Always give the person you ask a way to refuse. A reference may be uncomfortable saying no and may write a problematic letter, so preface your request with something like, "I know you are very busy right now. . . ," or "I need a strong recommendation for this position and wondered if you would have time to write one for me." Make sure all your references can meet the application deadline and send them necessary materials well ahead of time. Even a search committee that is enthusiastic about you may cool as they wait well past the deadline to receive your references. Find another reference if one of your references is uncertain about being able to be prompt. Send each reference a copy of the job description and ask if they would like copies of your *vita* or something to remind them of your accomplishments. You might also make suggestions for the angle you think it would be best for them to pursue with regard to your qualifications. A letter that specifically recommends you for a position is taken far more seriously than the general "to whom it may concern" type often found in placement files, so keep this in mind when asking your references for letters. Provide a stamped and addressed envelope for the letter writer.

Do not be afraid to ask for these letters. While your professors or employers may be busy, it is part of their responsibility to you and the profession to provide thoughtful references if they want you to succeed. Of course, to be fair, you should give them two weeks minimum to write a letter. The more lead time the better.

Check to see if your letters have arrived promptly by calling the search committee chair. If any are missing, gently prod the delinquent writer. A tactful approach may be "you probably already sent it, but it must be lost in the mail. I wonder if you could send another copy?"

Summary of I and II:
1. Tailor the cover letter to the advertised position.
2. Represent yourself accurately.
3. Use the letter to give information not in your *vita*.

4. Address the nature of the institution to which you are applying.
5. Keep the letter to under two pages.
6. Take great care in requesting letters of reference.
7. Make it as easy as possible for your references to write a good letter.
8. Check to make sure your letters of reference have arrived on time.

III. The *Curriculum vitae*

Spending a little time and money on a first-rate *vita* is worth the effort. If at all possible, either put it into a computer file yourself or pay someone to do it. Having it on computer makes revising and updating infinitely easier. In addition, the computer allows you to play with formatting and layout. Once you are ready to print final copy, use a laser printer for clean, sharp copies and use good quality bond or nice parchment paper. Some color other than white may help your *vita* stand out but be conservative in your choice of color: buff, soft gray or blue, beige, or ivory, or a paper such as parchment can suggest scholarly dignity. Colors such as pink, purple, goldenrod, red, etc. may trivialize your application in the minds of those whose style is more restrained.

The *vita* should include your full name and an address. Phone numbers are also helpful. Be sure to provide your employment history and current position. List your educational background. Put in all publications and professional activities and professional memberships. Listing your religious affiliation, age, marital status, and ethnicity are optional. If your citizenship might be challenged because of your name or country of origin, you might also list your citizenship and/or working visa status. Noting ethnicity is something of a tricky issue. If, as a woman of color, you do so, you may be interviewed simply to suit affirmative action guidelines at the institution. On the other hand, an institution sincerely seeking to diversify its faculty might be a welcome place to be if one is a woman of color, depending, of course, on actual support services. Some institutions have standing offers of a new position, if it can be filled by a person of color or an African American. How many clues you provide to your ethnicity is a practical and political choice that should be carefully considered.

As you work on your *vita*, there are several things to keep in mind. First, decide on categories that best present your experience and work. Also consider the order in which you will place those categories. If you have very little work experience, you may want to lead with your educational background. If you have received several awards for your work or during your education, create a category for awards and/or grants and scholarships and list them after your education. Unless the category is obvious, such as education, professional experience, and publications, it is best not to create a category unless you have at least two items to go under it, or better yet, three. If you have only one award, you might list it with the school you attended. A general enough category can include several things, such as awards/grants/fellowships, papers/panels, workshops, conferences, or professional development. Unless you are aiming for a seminary position, sermons and church activities are usually considered community activities, not professional work. Once you have taught several courses, list them, so a committee has some idea of what you are already prepared to teach. Some possible categories: committee assignments; courses taught; consulting and guest teaching; invited lectureships; informal, short, and non-scholarly writing; community service; additional education (such as international travel tours, continuing education, NEH summer seminars, etc.); and languages spoken, or studied. The important thing about categories is to make sure they make sense, give readers a picture of what you have done and who you are, and allow easy access to relevant information.

Second, be sure your categories are accurate. Do not place short, non-scholarly writing or book reviews in the same category as major essays. You will look as if you are misrepresenting yourself, or you will trivialize all your writing. People on search committees who are serious about your candidacy will often check your published material. Don't disappoint them. If you do not have enough published work to divide into categories, put all your items under the general category of publications, but give complete bibliographic references, including page numbers for the works, and list them from most to least major, rather than chronologically. List them chronologically when you have enough entries to create categories. (Note: It is important to list your published work in correct bibliographical form. It adds to your credibility as a scholar when your own *vita* demonstrates competency and attention to such details.)

A third thing to keep in mind is readability. When you formulate your categories, lay out the items so that important information is easy to see. For example, your current position, a chronological list of past positions (usually going from most to least recent), and the date of completion or anticipated completion of your degree, should be easy to find. If you don't trust your own visual sense, get someone who knows graphics to give you advice about layout or hire a professional resume preparer. You will want to select a good, readable typeface (sans serif is not a good idea because while it looks cleaner, it is harder to read) and leave enough white space to make reading easy on the eyes. A smaller typeface with more white space may be less difficult to read than a page crowded by large typeface.

Avoid over-formatting your *vita*. With a computer, you might be tempted to experiment with boxes or various fonts, but keep it simple and clean. Something you think is creative may look jumbled and busy to someone else.

Finally, you may want to have several versions of your *vita*: one that focuses on your religious activities for a seminary position; another that highlights your administrative experience for a job such as directing a women's studies program; a third that points to your scholarly and academic work for a university. If you have time in the application process, play with versions of your *vita* that are designed for the positions involved in your search.

Summary of III:
1. Put it on computer and take care to do a good job.
2. Decide what is essential and optional information.
3. Select categories with care.
4. Use accurate, comprehensive categories.
5. Make it clean and readable.
6. Create several versions.

CHAPTER TWO: INTERVIEWING

While the first few interviews for a job can seem formidable, it is important to remember that they are not like oral defenses or exams. You are not proving yourself or being grilled on your competence. You are participating in a mutual sharing of information that will help all parties concerned make the best decision possible for everyone involved. The less you regard the process as adversarial, the better it is likely to go. No matter how excellent your qualifications, they will not be the only factors considered by a search committee. Both you and your interviewers will be considering such intangibles as your "fit" with the department, colleagues with whom you may work closely for many years. They are as concerned as you are to get accurate information.

Remember that the interview process is to your benefit. You will want to investigate any institution for which you plan to work. You will spend many hours a day for possibly many years at this place and with your colleagues. It is important for you to find a good fit that will help you thrive as a scholar, teacher, and person. Look for signs that indicate institutional problems, for example, faculty apathy, polarized departmental camps, concern over budget cuts, bitter fighting among faculty, polemicized and antagonistic relationships between administration and faculty and/or students, and excessive burnout from overworked faculty. Trust your instincts about the integrity and straightforwardness of the administrators and faculty you meet. You may have to work with these people a long time.

I. Preliminary Preparation

Here are some important points to keep in mind:

A. <u>Do</u> <u>a</u> <u>lot</u> <u>of</u> <u>homework</u>.

In approaching your interview, there are several things to keep in mind. First, the more homework you do before you are interviewed, the better the interview is likely to go. A good interview requires that everyone involved prepare well. Your end of this involves a number of aspects, which are discussed below, but the more you know before you arrive, the more relaxed you are likely to be and the less likely you will get blindsided by unexpected news. If you are uncertain about the situation you are entering, your anxiety level is likely to be high, which may make you less animated and forthcoming than you ordinarily might be--behavior which could be interpreted as indifference to the job.

B. <u>Practice</u> <u>interviewing</u>.

One of the most helpful ways to prepare is to practice. Plan questions you may be asked and think up answers, or ask professors at your institution experienced at interviewing for suggestions about possible interview questions. Most <u>good</u> Career Planning and Placement Centers will conduct mock interviews and especially good centers will know types of interview questions to be encountered in different fields. You might also seek out new women faculty on your campus and ask them what the job hunt was like for them. An amusing--and de-mystifying--ploy is to have your friends role-play an interview with you, so you can rehearse. A case of interviewing anxiety can be helped when you imagine the formidable looking scholar facing you at your interview as your friend Amy, with a beard and pipe, grilling you the week before at your rehearsal.

C. <u>Investigate</u> <u>the</u> <u>institution</u>.

Be sure to investigate the character of the institution interviewing you. As stated above, there are many kinds of academic institutions from graduate schools to junior colleges to women's colleges to research-based to teaching-oriented. Each has its own distinctive needs and foci, and faculty concerns and responsibilities vary accordingly.

There are somewhat different strategies for the AAR/SBL placement interviews and on-site interviews, so they are discussed separately below. However, the skills and information gathered from one will be helpful to the other, so read both sections.

Summary of I:
  A. Do a lot of homework.
  B. Practice interviewing.
  C. Investigate the institution.

II.   AAR/SBL Placement Interviews

There is no way to describe these except as generally unpleasant and often grueling. The time is short and you are cast among hordes of job seekers. You usually have only about 30 minutes to make yourself stand out from what may be over 20 interviews conducted by a department, so keep the following in mind:

  A.   Register at the Placement Bureau and schedule carefully.

Make sure you are registered at the meeting with the locator file as soon as possible, so people can find you (there might be last minute scheduling changes or local shifts). Find out who will be on the interview team. Try to schedule your interviews with at least an hour in between. The breathing space gives you time to take notes on the interviews and to change locations if your interviews take place in different hotels. In addition, interviewers can get behind and delay your getting to your next appointment. Having your interviews well-spaced will help you be prompt.

  B.   Follow Placement Service Guidelines.

It is important to follow the Placement Service Guidelines, so study them. One important aspect of these interviews is location. Most take place at the stations provided by the Placement service. However, you may be asked to meet the search committee in another location. A meeting room, restaurant, or lounge area is acceptable, but it violates AAR/SBL placement policies to meet in a private hotel room or suite, and the Committee on the Status of Women in the Profession strongly advises against accepting invitations to interview in any such place.

The AAR/SBL Placement Assistance Center Job Interview Resolution policy states:

First, every job opportunity for which interviews are to be held at the Annual Meeting should be advertised in the November issue of OPENINGS.

Second, all interviews at the Annual Meeting, including interviews by pre-arranged appointments, should be conducted in space arranged by the PAC.

Third, no interviews are to be conducted in sleeping rooms.

Fourth, interviewees should be notified in a timely fashion of the location of the interviews.

Fifth, interviewers should communicate in writing to interviewees that, if they request to be interviewed in a different place, it will be arranged without prejudice to their candidacies.

Sixth, if any candidate requests within a reasonable time that an interview be moved to a different venue, the interviewers should make a good faith effort to comply, and notification should be given to the PAC staff that such a change was requested and what the disposition was.

Seventh, interviewees and interviewers are free to enlist the mediatorial services of the PAC staff in the event of differing views of what compliance with these guidelines entail.

Eighth, grievances of any kind regarding interviews conducted at the Annual Meeting may be filed with the AAR/SBL PAC, and will be referred to the PAC Advisory Committee for consideration.

The AAR and SBL, as sponsors of the PAC, provide space, professional personnel, materials, and highly advantageous room rental rates at the Annual Meeting. We respectfully request all who engage in the placement process at the Annual Meeting to cooperate with and participate in our efforts to create and maintain the highest professional service possible.

All institutions interviewing at the AAR/SBL should know about this rule, but, alas, many are ignorant of it or disregard it. As women in the profession, probably all of us have heard stories of sexual harassment and even sexual assault from women who were told to go to private rooms. All interviews in sleeping rooms violate placement guidelines. We suggest, if you really want an interview, you might graciously propose an alternative, more public location. For example, "Given the elevator wait in this hotel, I wonder if we could meet on a lower floor. I have an appointment immediately after this one, and I am concerned about making it on time without cutting short my time with your committee," or "I have to be at a paper immediately after my interview, and I am concerned about making it on time," or "Could we meet in a more accessible location. With these elevators, going up and down to the 26th floor will add 5 or 10 minutes to my transit time, which is time I would rather spend with your committee."

If you are asked to attend an interview in a room that violates placement policies, you should seek to arrange an alternative location as soon as possible. Do not wait until the last minute. Take care of it immediately. Your odds of getting an alternative location are much higher if you give the search committee time to find an alternative site and to notify other interviewees.

There are pros and cons about mentioning the AAR/SBL policy directly. It is printed periodically in Openings, but not all scholars subscribe to it. Those who do may not have noticed the policy. In cases of ignorance, a search committee may appreciate your calling it to their attention, gently. After all, the policy also protects them from suspicion of impropriety. On the other hand, your interviewers may have chosen to disregard this policy. If you point out the policy, and they explain they are disregarding it, it is fair to ask for an explanation and/or another location. Neither request is likely to win you points. You may, however, want to consider the underlying message about attitudes toward sexual harassment conveyed by a search committee that chooses to disregard the policy. You ought to consider reporting violators of the policy to the AAR/SBL Placement Services Office. If you are not sure, ask the advice of someone you trust at the meeting.

C. At the interview you should be ready to:

1. Summarize your dissertation in 2 to 5 minutes and be prepared to elaborate for another 5, if asked. Don't just describe the topic, but state the main thesis and arguments, theoretical content, methodological approach, and explain its scholarly importance (don't sell yourself short here). Do not state anything apologetically or negatively and hold forth with some enthusiasm.

2. Be able to demonstrate that you are aware of developments and movements in your field beyond your dissertation. It is important to show you understand your field and can place yourself within its various trends. You might also use a discussion of your dissertation to explain its larger implications.

3. Be able to state your long term research interests, whether they directly relate to your dissertation, or move into other areas. Don't be hesitant to set some of the agenda for discussion yourself and to take the initiative in presenting your interests.

4. Be prepared to talk about your teaching successes, if you have had some experience there. Discuss your teaching interests, as well as the kind of courses you would like to teach, courses that suit your training and interests and that would enhance and supplement their current offerings (it helps to be familiar with their already existing curriculum when making such suggestions).

5. Show that you know or have learned something about the interviewing institution and department if at all possible.

6. Be able to describe your criteria for a good or fitting position for you and describe your professional objectives as they are relevant to that institution.

D.   Project confidence and a friendly, collegial style.

Whether you actually feel it or not, try to project a note of confidence (not braggadocio).   Deference in women is a traditional expectation, but what most male scholars are seeking is a colleague who can "hold her own" with the "boys." Holding your own means not being afraid to voice real opinions and discussing them thoughtfully, or even passionately, if the topic warrants. It also means not dodging thought-provoking questions, and asking a few yourself, if there is time.

Your potential colleagues will want to see if you are collegial and will make a good addition to their department. Conveying a friendly, collegial style indicates your approachability and willingness to be part of a community of scholars. However, in attempting to be friendly take care not to seem giddy, trivial, seductive or silly.

E.   Find out search timeline.

Be sure you know the search committee's timeline and ask when you should expect to be called for an interview, if that is their decision. If you don't hear by that date, wait a few days (to account for unexpected delays on their end) and call them.

One hint: if the search committee spends a lot of time telling you about their institution and seems to be drawing your interest to it, that is usually a good sign. Don't let them, however, take up too much of the time you have for presenting yourself. It can seem like a relief if they want to do all the talking, but at the end of the time, they will not have gotten to know you much better.

Summary of II:

A.   Register at the Placement Bureau and schedule carefully.
B.   Follow Placement service guidelines.
C.   At the interview you should be ready to talk about your work, your field, and your current research.

16

D. Project confidence and a friendly, collegial style.
E. Find out search timeline.

III. On-Site Interviews

If you are asked to interview on-site, the odds are good that you are on a short list for this position. Extra preparation before you arrive for the interview will help your confidence level and impress your interviewers, so invest some time paving your way to the campus visit. There are many aspects to an on-site interview, which are covered individually below.

Find out how travel expenses will be covered. You needn't ask immediately, but ask at some point late in the conversation about your visit. If the interviewing institution is not paying your expenses, it is likely they are interviewing many candidates and your chances of getting the job will be lessened. Some financially strapped institutions will pay your expenses if you accept the job or if you are not offered the job. In this case, if you are offered the job and don't take it, you have to pay your own expenses. In a deal like this, you may arrive on campus and discover that the job is wrong for you, which means you are out expenses if they offer it to you. In such circumstances you can, of course, conduct such a rotten interview that the odds are lowered of your being offered the job. This last tactic, while saving you money, may be a little risky. Acquaintances at schools do talk about people they have interviewed and you may be maligned.

A. Preparation for an on-site interview:
   1. Find out about potential colleagues and department.
   Find out about members of the department(s) interviewing you and read what they have written. Knowing their strengths and research interests will help you talk to them. Also read catalogue information about the institution and the department(s) interviewing you. Shape your questions to this specific information, such

as curriculum, general education requirements, and department requirements.

2. Be prepared for varieties of interviewers.

You are likely to be interviewed by students, faculty outside the department, or administrators who are less familiar with your credentials, so be prepared to give nutshell versions of your work for those who have not read your dossier or publications. This is important because even members of search committees may need a reminder. They will have read many dossiers and might welcome information from you.

3. Find out performance expectations and prepare.

Find out if this is to be a preliminary or full interview. Some institutions conduct two levels of interviews to screen applicants. Ask if you will be expected to present a public lecture or conduct a class. Ask about audience size and makeup, type of room, and the expected length of the talk. Practice your lecture with friends so it is the right length and sufficiently engaging to hold the attention of the audience. Reading a text out loud beforehand is important. Things that read well silently often sound dry or dull out loud. A search committee may tell you they want to discuss your work with you informally. Take along a paper anyway, even if you use it just for notes. It never hurts to have a text for backup in case you draw a blank or get stage fright. They might also change their minds and ask for something more formal.

4. Consider sending extra materials, if necessary.

A search committee interested in you will probably look up your published work, or ask you to send it. However, if the request for application materials in the position advertisement does not ask for more than a *vita* and references, you might carefully consider enclosing a little bit extra. For example, if the job description calls for teaching an introductory course in your field, you might enclose a syllabus from such a course that you have already taught. Be sure it is a thorough, carefully prepared syllabus. If you have a particular essay that has received praise from your colleagues or professors, you might send the search committee a copy. But keep such enclosures to a minimum and carefully select them. Well-presented material that helps a search committee know you better before you arrive can be helpful if the material is of excellent quality.

5.   Arrange to meet various campus groups.

The search committee may ask you if there is any particular campus group you would like to meet. If they have not scheduled it, ask to see student majors and minors in your discipline. If you also work in women's studies and/or an ethnic studies program, ask to meet with majors and minors or with students who may work in the women's or ethnic studies centers. Try to meet with other women faculty and faculty of color (especially if you are a woman of color). Their opinions are likely to count for a lot. The same is not generally true, however, if you are a lesbian wanting to meet gay and lesbian faculty. Coming out about your sexuality is a very personal decision that, given the pervasiveness of homophobia, may cost you the job. It is appropriate, however, for both heterosexuals and gays and lesbians to ask to meet with student or faculty groups that advocate the rights of gays and lesbians. In requesting such meetings, you will need to weigh the risks involved in terms of the climate at the institution interviewing you.

6.   Discuss salary late in the process.

At some point late in the interview process, there should be a discussion of salary and benefits. This may be with a dean, department head, or search committee chair. Do not bring this up when meeting with the department, a group, or with the whole search committee. Usually some administrator with budget responsibilities, such as the Dean, will be the one to discuss salary. Be sure you have done your homework on the kinds of salary range this institution offers. Academe, the journal of the American Association of University Professors (AAUP), annually publishes a list of college and university salaries by area of the country, rank, and discipline area or field, including benefit packages (Academe, Suite 500, 1012 14th St., N. W., Washington, D.C. 20005). If you know someone who held the job before you or trust someone in the department for good information, ask what a reasonable salary should be. Find out the criteria used to assess rank and make sure the rank you are offered is fair (rank affects salary). If you know what you should expect, it will help you in negotiating a good salary. A good time to ask about salary if no one has raised the issue is during the last meeting with the dean, department chair, or search committee chair. Some schools do not negotiate salaries because they pay everyone equally at a particular rank. Try to find out what the policy is for the institution.

7.   Investigate benefits.

In addition to salary, you should also look at the benefits they offer and ask about the total package (total of salary plus benefits). For example, many institutions offer TIAA-CREF pension payments, with a monthly payment of 5-10% of your salary, beyond the salary they pay you. Some institutions require you to pay an additional percentage out of your gross salary. Many seminaries and church-related colleges and universities use denominational pension plans. Investigate these and see if you have an option to choose a company. Pension benefits are an important consideration because, unless you plan to stay at a denominational school most of your career, you may have to change companies midstream and be unable to cash out an account or collect anything until retirement, or until you are fully vested, which can take years. Types of medical coverage are also important. If you have the option and are relatively young and healthy, you should consider a Health Maintenance Organization (HMO) plan, if it is offered. These take care of routine exams and regular preventive health care at virtually no cost, an important consideration if you are just starting full-time work. If you have or are planning to have children or expect to care for aging parents, investigate family leave policies and check on the availability of child care. (More on this in the Maternity section.) Check also on disability and life insurance. Dental insurance is an added perk that is not universally offered.

8. Ask about computers.

Ask about computer facilities and the backup computing help offered by the institution. Universities and colleges with computer science departments and labs usually offer fairly complete services. Many institutions provide computers for faculty. If a computer is not offered, see if you can negotiate one as part of your package. Even if you own one that you use at home, you will want one at your office, especially if your personal one is not compatible with the system used at the institution. An institution should be willing to provide you with office computer equipment because it is in their interest to support your work as a scholar and teacher.

9.   Don't rush into an offer.

If your interview includes a discussion of salary and benefits, don't hesitate to get full information about the job offer. Also, it is all right to let them know you are being interviewed for other positions, as long as you do not misrepresent yourself. Don't be afraid to ask for more than you are offered, within the range of salaries offered at your rank in that department. There is more play in what an institution can offer than most new Ph.D.'s know. If a place wants you enough, they can sometimes make a deal. You will rarely be expected to accept an offer at your interview, but if this happens, it is entirely acceptable to say that you need time to think it over and will get back to them. Ask for the offer in writing before you accept; stay in control of the process.

Summary of III. A.:

1.   Find out about potential colleagues and department.
2.   Be prepared for varieties of interviewers.
3.   Find out performance expectations and prepare.
4.   Send extra materials.
5.   Arrange to meet various campus groups.
6.   Prepare to discuss salary late in the process.
7.   Investigate benefits.
8.   Ask about computers.
9.   Don't rush into an offer.

B.   At the interview:
     1.   Get a clear schedule.
     Check the schedule for your interview and make sure you have been given sufficient rest breaks. If you do not receive a typed agenda, ask for one. How many breaks and how long you want them depends on your needs, but don't be

hesitant to ask for an occasional breather if the search committee has been so unkind as to schedule back to back appointments all day plus a dinner in the evening. You are likely to be taken to several meals, including a dinner at a nice restaurant. The dinner is often a way for the committee to show off the local community by taking you to an exceptional place. If you are worried about what to order because you don't want to appear extravagant or cheap, ask those at your table to recommend the house specialty or the best thing on the menu. It gives them a chance to brag and you a chance to get an idea of what to order. If you have special food needs, it is helpful to let people know at the time your schedule is arranged.

2.   Think about where you are positioned in an interview.

When you are offered a choice of places to sit at an interview, think about the chair you will use. You do not want a deep, plush chair that puts you lower than everyone else or that makes you sit awkwardly, or too far back. You want a chair that is comfortable, but keeps you forward and alert, at eye level with everyone else. It is also probably better to sit where you can see the door. If people come in late you will be able to see them. Being able to see everyone in the room gives you greater command over the logistics, and you will be able to maintain eye contact with everyone. If you are offered a chair you do not like, there is nothing wrong with asking if you can use a different one.

3.   Pay attention to appearance and comfort.

Dress is very much a personal issue, but, as with all forms of human behavior, it sends certain cultural codes and signals. It is important to think what your colleagues are likely to read into your physical appearance. While academic life allows for a great deal more idiosyncracy than many other learned professions, there are probably certain danger areas you should avoid at an interview. Clothing too tight or too short will seem unprofessional. Many women (including potential colleagues) are likely to think you are trying to seduce your way into the job, and academic men are often uncomfortable with too much explicit heterosexuality. The issue of appropriate dress is especially important for women of color who bear the double burden of racial stereotypes and assumptions. Given that many of these stereotypes have to do with loose sexual mores and behaviors, it is important that you project an image of professionalism and dignity. If you are unsure of what to wear, observe what other women in the profession seem to be wearing, or ask a female professor in your department for advice.

Select clothing that is comfortable and convenient. This is not the time to wear a blouse that keeps coming untucked or a skirt that twists around. Clothing that does not wrinkle in transit will save one layer of stress when you arrive. Pockets in your clothes are helpful; they give you a place to put nervous hands when lecturing and storage for small items like tissues or contact lens drops. Carry an extra pair of nylons in your purse. Think about whether you tend to be too warm when nervous or especially cold. Sweating because you dressed too warmly or shaking everyone's hands with icy fingers can be unsettling. Dress to give yourself some flexibility for internal and external climates, such as layering, rather than wearing one heavy sweater. It is also advisable to either wear or carry comfortable shoes. Campuses are often large, and you may find yourself walking long distances; do not add aching feet to interview jitters.

In addition to clothing, body language is an important part of self-presentation. Be sure you look people in the eye when speaking to them and make frequent, direct, friendly eye contact. If you are speaking to a group, look around and make eye contact with each person.

Summary of III. B.:

1. Get a clear schedule.
2. Think about where you are positioned in an interview.
3. Pay attention to appearance and comfort.

    C.   Teaching Audition:

        1.   Get advance materials ready.

If you are asked to teach a class, get a syllabus for the course ahead of time and be sure you will have any media equipment you might need. You may also want to send a text for students to have read in advance, or use the reading from the syllabus to set what you teach.

        2.   Warm up students.

To enhance your interactions with students and to demonstrate your teaching (not lecturing) skills, there are techniques for drawing out the students so that they will interact with you more and be responsive. If you have time, have each student introduce her/himself to you with a name and some information like college major or religious upbringing, etc. Remember to share something about yourself, beyond your credentials. Discrete self-disclosure can be disarming and help students feel comfortable with you. Creating a sense of community, however you can do it, will make your reception much more positive.

        3.   Help students be actively involved.

Another technique might be called "priming the pump." Do not launch into your lecture first. Beginning with lecture tends to make students quiet and passive, especially with a guest. Instead, begin with a question that leads them toward the topic of your lecture, but invites them to speculate on the subject, and go clear around the room, if the class is small enough (this can be combined with introductions). If the class is large, have all the students write a reflection on your question, just for a few minutes. Then ask for volunteers to share what they wrote. Call on students if no one volunteers.

This process serves at least two functions. Students listen better when they have a vested interest. An example of such a question might be, "what has puzzled you the most this semester as you have studied religion (ethics, the role of women in religion, sacred texts, etc.) Priming the pump gets students used to talking, so that they are more likely to interact with you through the lecture or at the end when you ask for questions. It also lets you collect some students' thinking on the topic, and, if you are quick on your feet, you can comment on what they said as you lecture and tie your content to their concerns. Do not use their opening comments to correct them (it is best to select a question that has no right or wrong answer, but is interesting for speculation). If you have to, ignore incorrect comments and stay with the helpful ones, or do your correcting very respectfully. If you don't tie their comments into your lecture, discuss them with the students afterward or briefly before.

If you are just too nervous to interact with students at first, or you prefer to lecture right away, leave yourself at least 10-15 minutes at the end. After you finish, if the students are silent or ask few questions, ask them to use five minutes to write a summary of the important points of your lecture in a paragraph or two, or ask them to write five questions that cannot be answered directly from your lecture content, but might be answerable with some outside research. Have them share their summaries, writing the main points on the board as they report them, or ask them to share their questions and discuss them. The students are likely to be impressed with your range of knowledge on the topic, if you are able to answer some of their questions. They will also be impressed if you applaud the difficult and interesting nature of a question you cannot answer.

4.   Pitch your lecture at the right level.

If you are to teach or lecture to an undergraduate class-- especially an intro class (which is often what new faculty are

26

asked to teach)--make it accessible. Avoid the esoteric or technical. If you present work from your dissertation, be sure to think about your audience. It is possible to sound authoritative without being arrogant. A paper that netted an "A" in a graduate course may get you an "F" from intro students. Student evaluations from these teaching auditions are often included in the search committee's materials, especially at teaching-oriented institutions. You might ask someone who represents a member of your target audience to go over your presentation with you. With the shortage of college students at financially strapped institutions, many formerly research-oriented places are taking a second look at effective teaching. Helpful background reading is the chapter on "Connected Teaching" in <u>Women's</u> <u>Ways</u> <u>of</u> <u>Knowing</u>, Mary Field Belenky, Blythe McVicker Clinchy, Nancy Rule Goldberger, and Jill Mattuck Tarule, New York: Harper & Row, 1986.

<u>Summary</u> <u>of</u> <u>III.</u> <u>C.</u>:
1. Get advance materials ready.
2. Warm up students.
3. Help students be actively involved.
4. Pitch your lecture at the right level.

D. <u>Handling</u> <u>Tough</u> <u>Questions:</u>
Using information about your marital status, race, religion, sex, age, and sexual orientation to deny you a job is illegal. Unfortunately, once a search committee learns personal information about you, it is often impossible to prove such information was the basis of your being turned down. Hence, how you handle such questions is determined by many factors: how badly you need the job, whether you think the question is asked in innocent ignorance, and how willing you are to share details about your private life. It is best to plan out your responses to this type of question ahead of time. Weigh the risks involved in various responses. You will probably not be offered the job if you accuse the search committee

of illegal behavior. Artful dodges may be more effective evasive maneuvers. One caution: interviewers may try other ways besides direct questions to gather personal information about you. For example, at a social gathering, they may use informal conversation to draw you out (a good reason to limit your alcohol intake), or, if they have a woman in the department, they may ask her about information you may have shared casually in private conversation. Decide how much you are going to share and don't offer more to anyone in any situation if you want the information kept private. On the other hand, don't be afraid to let them know you are a real person with nonacademic interests. There are plenty of neutral areas for self-disclosure, such as tastes in music, books, physical activities, travel, etc.

The field of religion is somewhat different from other fields in that your religious affiliation may be part of your eligibility for a job, especially at seminaries and church-related schools. In these situations, it is not illegal for an institution to use religion as a criterion for employment.

1. Possible answers to questions about your partner or children:
    a) "I have no commitments that would prevent me from taking this job."
    b) "I'm not sure you want to be asking me that question" (stated in a pleasant tone of voice).

    Pause while they think about why you said that.

    If they ask why, you might gently explain to them that the use of such information for job eligibility is illegal, and while you don't mind answering, they should be aware that it is not an appropriate question. You might also think up a more amusing response to the why question. One woman was asked how she was going to be able to keep her house clean with all the responsibilities of the new job. When they asked why they shouldn't be asking her, she replied, "because you are assuming it is clean now and that it will get dirtier."

2. <u>Age and race questions:</u>

These may be handled by explaining the inappropriateness of the question, or with humor.

a) "Well, I'm probably older than I look, but only my hairdresser knows for sure."

b) "This is the Chinese year of the tiger, and I was born in the year of the tiger, which means I am either 12, 24, 36, 48 or 60."

c) "One reason I didn't become a mathematician is that I've never been good at exact numbers."

It may be helpful to be kind but firm about racial questions, which tend to be seen as the most taboo.

d) "I wasn't aware there was a racial qualification for this position."

e) "Will my race make a difference to my candidacy for this position?"

3. <u>Ask your friends, colleagues, or professors for suggestions about appropriate ways to handle such questions.</u>

The main thing is not to get caught off guard by such questions or to come across as a hostile or "rabid" radical in your refusals to answer. If you know certain questions will set off a negative reaction in you, practice keeping your cool and creating gracious, tactful, friendly strategies.

4. <u>Discrimination may not be as overt as an inappropriate question, but it may occur nonetheless.</u>

For example, an innocent sounding comment like "this town is a good place to raise a family" or "this community is traditional and rural" may imply that gays and lesbians or Blacks/Jews/Hispanics/Asians are not welcome. Innuendos are often hard to detect, and such comments can be simply a realistic assessment of the situation. On the other hand, they may be codes for racism, sexism, homophobia, ageism, or ableism. If you suspect a hidden message, it may be helpful to put it out in the open, or you may decide you would prefer not to have such a person as a colleague.

5.   Handle <u>awkward</u> <u>interviewers</u> <u>carefully.</u>

Most interviewers are eager to put you at ease, but there will be those who seem to regard interviewing as hazing and who seek to heighten stress levels. If you are feeling badgered, stay aware of your feelings and react with as much poise and self-control as you can. Whether you choose to fight back, deflect the hostility with humor or graciousness, or walk out, do your best to preserve your dignity. Remember, too, that some scholars' interactive style is combative, and they value such confrontation. They may not mean anything personal by coming across as abrasive or hostile, so it will work to your advantage not to take such treatment personally.

At the opposite end from the bully or harasser is the overly friendly, accommodating interviewer. He or she may seem especially eager to give you inside information, to act as a strong advocate for you, or to bend over backward to make him or herself available to you. If this is someone you do not know personally, be cordial, but careful. You could be in the position of being entrapped in a no-win situation. A faculty member who perceives him or herself as an outsider to a department, as someone who is marginalized or victimized by her or his colleagues, may have already latched on to you as an ally against the others. Do not ask for inappropriate information and be cautious about letting others think that your relationship to this person is any more than it is. If you feel inappropriate boundaries are being crossed, trust those feelings. If others in the department misperceive the two of you as good friends, you may have your candidacy undermined by the department's antagonism toward their colleague, especially if no one else in the department knows you. Having an inside track with someone like this is usually not an advantage.

6. Special Issues Affecting Women of Color

    a)   "I see you have a Ph.D in Systematic Theology from Harvard Divinity School, but I'm wondering if you would feel comfortable teaching students about the Nicene Creed?"

    b)   "I see your dissertation was on Black and Third World Theologies, do you know anything about the Reformation?"

    c)   "You do know that you will be teaching more than Black students, do you think you can handle that?"

    d)   "We're really impressed by how well you use the language. You are so articulate."

    e)   "We've really been impressed by your ability to develop a logical argument so spontaneously."

In spite of the good intentions of the interviewers, the chances are that who you are as a woman of color will elicit "peculiar" competency tests and gratuitous comments concerning your intellect. The religious academy is not free from the cultural biases, prejudices, and limitations of American society. It is an exception when the interview process is free from them. So once again, as a person of color you will carry an unfair double burden into the interview setting. You must deal with the typical expectations of a job interview, and you must navigate the mine-field of stereotypes and prejudices heaped upon you because of your ethnicity or race. There are several ways in which you might deal with the insulting and patronizing remarks you are likely to face.

You may first choose not to place yourself in what may be a dehumanizing and demeaning situation. In order to make this decision, it is important to investigate the institution prior to your interview. You should find out about the ethnic and racial composition of its faculty, staff, and students.

Find ways to speak with people of color associated with the institution. Ask questions concerning the experiences of those persons. Carefully review the institution's curriculum. Are there academic requirements which insure that students encounter the viewpoints of persons from various ethnic and cultural groups? Will you be able to teach courses from your own area of interests? How will those courses be viewed in the overall educational objectives of the institution? Will, for instance, they be considered integral to the school's curriculum or superfluous?

How well informed you are about the institution will help you to determine whether or not the institution is a place you think you want to be as a scholar. You may have to decide how much "racism" you can tolerate in your work environment. If you are certain that the institution is not a place where you can thrive as a teacher and scholar, then you might withdraw from the process and avoid a potentially abusive interview situation.

If you do decide to become a part of the interview process, you should develop some strategy prior to the interview for dealing with offensive statements. Your degree of interest in the position, of course, will dictate the strategy which you adopt. Ask your friends and colleagues for suggestions in dealing with racist questions and comments. The following are some possible responses:

To questions about your competency: ask your interviewer if there is anything about your *vita* that raises concerns about your ability to teach in the area in which you have been trained.

To remarks of "amazement" concerning your intellectual abilities: you might comment, "I take it from your remark that you have had a number of well-trained scholars who are not articulate and cannot think logically;" or ask why they would be so shocked that an eminently trained scholar would possess these skills. You may also want to point out that their amazement says more about them and their prejudices than it does about you and your abilities.

Finally, you may want to inform them of the racist nature of their questions and comments and inquire if these biases are typical of other faculty or administrators at the institution.

Essentially, it is important that you handle the situation the way in which you are most comfortable. Remember, however, that the interviewers are representative of their institution. Do not expect their biases and prejudices to be an exception to what you will encounter if you accept the position at that particular institution.

If you have any interest in the position at all, it is very important that you keep a clear and detailed record of all contact that you have had with the institution. This record will be vital if you find it necessary at any point in your involvement with the institution to file suit against it for ethnic or racial discrimination.

7.   Special Issues Affecting Lesbians

Questions about family status that might be awkward and uncomfortable for all women can be especially difficult for lesbians. The decision as to whether and how to come out at an interview is a very personal one that each lesbian must make herself. Sometimes you know in advance that coming out would cost you the job--e.g. at certain church-related institutions--or that it would be very difficult to be at a particular institution as a lesbian. Unless you have political reasons for going through the interview process--e.g., it is your church, and you are committed to changing its policies--there is probably no reason to put yourself in such a situation.

In general, however, it is probably fair to say that colleagues or potential colleagues are more likely to take your lesbianism in stride if they know and respect you already than if they are meeting you for the first time. This is an argument for not coming out at an interview but for taking your time to get the feel of an institution after you have a job. On the other hand, if you are used to being entirely out in every area of your life and could not imagine accepting a job were your colleagues not comfortable with your lesbianism, you might want to use the opportunity provided by an inappropriate question to talk about your household arrangements!

Decisions about whether and how to come out in relation to the job search actually begin before the interviewing process, when you are preparing a *vita*. Should you include those articles in gay and lesbian anthologies or that piece in a gay periodical on your list of publications? Do you want to mention your membership on the steering committee of a gay organization or your gay community service? Again, depending on the kind of job you are looking for and how out you are in the rest of your life, you might want to exclude such references entirely or use them as a gentle probe to get some feeling for the openness of the places where you are considering positions. You have to consider, of course, that this may mean there will be institutions that will rule you out at the first stage of reading applications.

If you do choose to include signals of lesbian involvement on your *vita*, you cannot then make any assumptions as to how these will be read! Some places will assume that anyone who does lesbian-related research or is involved in any gay-related organization is a lesbian, whether or not that is true. Other places may fail to make what are to you, obvious connections. Sometimes women who have done a lot of writing or speaking about lesbian issues just assume that potential employers will know from their *vita* that they are gay. But if it is important to you that an institution does know before it hires you, you cannot count on their figuring it out themselves. We know a feminist who has done extensive work on lesbian issues, whose *vita* lists lots of lesbian involvements, and who just assumed when she was offered a job that the department knew she was a lesbian. Though it turned out not to matter in the end, she was very startled to discover after several months that her chairperson in fact had no idea.

There is still another twist, of course, to the coming out issue. If you are out as a graduate student, but want to take your time coming out at a new institution, you have to be prepared for the fact that your interviewers may have learned through the grapevine that you are a lesbian. Obviously, if they do not eliminate you for this reason but choose to invite you to the institution for an interview anyway, your being a lesbian should not prevent you from getting the job. But as most lesbians are all too aware, one can spend a lot of time agonizing over whether to come out only to discover that the choice is not in one's hands.

If you do feel that you were not considered for a job because of your sexuality--and you may sometimes have that hunch or even get feedback from friends at an institution--there is generally little you can do about it. The selection process is sufficiently amorphous at its early stages that there is very little documentation and many ways an institution can cover itself--assuming that sexual orientation is even a protected category. Just focus on the jobs that don't rule you out--and keep on working for wider social change.

An issue that sometimes comes up for lesbians at job interviews and that is very difficult to know how to handle is the issue of self-presentation. We know of a couple of cases in which male members of departments were very disturbed and disconcerted after interviewing a lesbian because she did not respond at all to low level sexual signals or play any of the subtle games that surround male/female interaction. Of course, the men did not articulate the issue this way but simply said the woman was unfriendly or would not be a good colleague. If you have a "dykey" self-presentation, there is probably no way to rule out this kind of response. It can be helpful, however, to realize what is going on if a member of the search committee seems to be reacting strangely. All you can do is present yourself in the best light, stressing your credentials as a potential teacher and scholar, and perhaps highlighting some of the ways you have functioned as an effective colleague in the graduate school setting.

Summary of III. D.:

1. Handle age, race, and lifestyle questions very carefully.
2. Be careful of overly combative or excessively friendly interviewers.
3. Be extra alert to racist cues if you are a woman of color, or homophobic ones if you are a lesbian.
4. Consider carefully how you will react to racism.
5. Don't assume a department will or will not know your sexual orientation, but think about how you will come out, if you choose to do so.

E.   Do not react rashly to harassment.

If you are confronted with sexual harassment, racism, or with illegal questions, you will need to consider your options. To let it pass may not be wise, but to react especially strongly will probably sabotage your chances at the job. In addition, if you are seeking your first position and you create a fuss, you may be labeled a trouble-maker. If the behavior is beyond innocent ignorance, you should consider a letter to the person's supervisor, dean, or president or even legal action, especially if you have accepted another position. Whatever you decide to do, be sure, if you suspect anything amiss, to write everything down that is said and done to you. If you take legal action, it will strengthen your case considerably to have an accurate log of events and statements written down close to the occurrence of those events. Talk over your options at home with a support group, friend, attorney, and/or affirmative action officer/ombudsperson, etc. before you act. Useful advice and moral support will be important if you decide to begin a grievance process that may be painful and protracted.

<u>Summary of III. E.</u>:
1. Do not react rashly to sexual harassment and get good advice before acting.

F. <u>Questions you should ask at the interview</u>:
Some of the following information may be volunteered before you ask, but if it isn't, ask. <u>And write down everything you are told.</u> Have a list of questions to ask. It shows you are interested in knowing more about the institution and your colleagues.

1. <u>Questions about the job demands and support services.</u>
Be sure you are clear about payment for relocation expenses. When you are negotiating the offer, try to get these paid in full. Some institutions will pay them only if you are moving from one academic position to another. Others have a sliding scale based on the distance of your move. Still others pay only a set maximum amount. When you are moving from graduate student to faculty, the expense of a major move is not a welcome one. Avoid paying for the move with credit cards, if you can. Find out if your hiring institution will give you a low interest loan, or will give you a salary advance that can be paid off in installments.

Ask about teaching load, maximum class size (if there is a cap on registrations for classes), opportunities for development of new courses, the number of undergraduates in a class that earns you a teaching/research assistant, examination policies, equipment resources (especially computers), student/graduate thesis advising, committee responsibilities, size and location of your office, secretarial help, other support services, support for professional development for research and publishing as well as teaching, travel allowances for meetings, policies about leave time and sabbaticals, tenure, promotion, and evaluation procedures, department structure, the political and committee structure of the faculty, and library facilities (ask for a tour of the religion section).

2.   Questions about the climate of an institution.

To collect clues about the culture of an institution, ask about such things as the administration's and faculty's views of the institution's distinctive character. Ask what three biggest challenges the institution faces in the next five years and ask what was its most significant crisis of the past ten years. You might also question members of the department about the characteristics they most value in a colleague.

3.   Questions of a more general nature.

There are also general issues in higher education that you can ask, such as how well funded the institution is, the average class size, how salary increases are determined and whether they are regular, how fractious the overall faculty is, the percentage of women and people of color on the faculty and in the student body, what the relationship to the religious body is (if it is church-related) and what encouragement there is for interdisciplinary work or team teaching. Students are often willing to talk about key issues and the latest controversies on campus. They can be a good source of inside information. Ask faculty about the history of the institution, about the kind of students who attend and their strengths and weaknesses.

4.   Questions about the community.

Ask about the community you will live in and the cost of living. Many search committees will give you a tour of the town. If there is time, ask for one. If not, ask a lot of questions about the kind of place it is, its governance structures, its recreational opportunities, its arts and schools, etc. Be sure to buy at least one local paper. It will give you some idea of housing costs.

Summary of III. F.:

1. Ask questions about the job demands and support services.
2. Ask questions about the climate of an institution.
3. Ask questions of a more general nature.
4. Ask questions about the community.

G. Miscellaneous Items to Keep in Mind

1. Keep a log of your applications.

If you are sending out many applications, keep track of them by logging them somewhere, noting exactly when and what items were sent out in each application, filing any requests for additional information, and listing contact persons with notes on any phone conversations.

2. Phone interviews.

Some institutions make use of phone interviews. If you will be interviewed by phone, be sure they let you know ahead of time. If they call unexpectedly, you should ask to reschedule. Ask who will be present at the phone interview and be prepared with all the notes you will need for the interview. While it can be unsettling to talk to strangers you cannot see, the advantage of a phone interview is that you can take notes all through the conversation to keep track of things. These interviews can be quite lengthy, so when you schedule, get some idea of the time frame involved.

The disadvantage of phone interviews is that information one gets from talking face to face is lost. You will have no visual clues and neither will the search committee. If you have a soft speaking voice, be sure to speak up. If you are on a speaker, speaking clearly and loudly enough is important. If you tend to have a flat speaking style, you should concentrate on animating it more. Strive to sound interesting and competent.

3.   Items to take along.

Carry copies of your *vita* and other materials with you to interviews, especially at AAR/SBL. It is much better to be able to give them upon request than to promise to send them later.

4.   Handling uninterested interviewers.

You may encounter an interviewer who seems to have no real interest in you, which is possible for a number of reasons. Another candidate may have emerged earlier as the favorite or there may be someone from the inside in first place. You may been interviewed only for affirmative action reasons. The department may be deeply divided about the candidate it wants. Regardless of the disinterest, do your best and do not express disappointment, anger, or bitterness. The top candidate may withdraw or go elsewhere, another position may open up, or you may run into the interviewer elsewhere who will remember you favorably. If nothing else, you can use the interview for practice and see how well you can do, or try some risky things to see how they fly.

5.   Follow-up to the interview.

Some people write thank-you notes to chairs of departments and/or search committees for on-site interviews. These probably don't hurt and can give you a chance to reiterate your interest in the position and to add a point about yourself that you didn't have a chance to mention at the interview ("I enjoyed teaching xyz class. It was very much like one for which I developed a study packet of materials here at abc university," or "I appreciated the opportunity to speak to your women's studies program and to learn that they are involved in the development of a sexual harassment policy, a process very similar to one I assisted here at abc university last year").

6.   Review the interview.

After you complete an interview, take notes on what happened, especially on what you would like to improve. Writing a record while the interview is fresh in your mind will help you keep details straight and improve the next one, if you are not offered this position.

Summary of III. G:
1.   Keep a log of your applications.
2.   Carry extra copies of your *vita* to interviews.
3.   Don't be unnerved by an apathetic interviewer.
4.   Follow-up with thank-you notes.
5.   Review the interview to see where you can improve.

Final Summary of Key Points
1.   Be positive about yourself, your interviewers, and the institution interviewing you.
2.   Be prepared with answers to obvious questions.
3.   Be prepared to ask questions of your own, especially about things that concern you.
4.   Keep your cool and focus on surviving with your dignity intact if things go wrong.
5.   Keep good notes on your interviews.
6.   Go over your interview afterward to see how you might improve.

CHAPTER THREE: NEGOTIATING AN OFFER

Congratulations! If you are reading this section seriously, it means you have been offered the job. There are no magic or perfect ways to negotiate an offer. You should, at the outset, find out what the time limit is for making a decision (a week is reasonable). You will need to trust your instincts about how far to push negotiations. Many women enter a job negotiation with the attitude that they do not deserve any money so they feel grateful for whatever they are offered. This is not the time to hold onto a self-sacrificing and self-effacing attitude. You should have strong reasons for arguing your case in a negotiation. If you have been offered a position, it usually means they want you and want you to be happy. You should expect to be treated fairly from the outset. Often, if a department is excited about hiring you, your willingness to negotiate for more may give them some leverage to go to the administration and to ask for more. If you know anyone on the search committee who can give you a sense of how strong your bargaining position is, you may find out you are in a very good position to negotiate.

It is crucial to have done your homework about the salary range offered by the institution and criteria for ranking faculty. You should also have collected information at your interview about relocation reimbursements. In addition, you should know the total "package" offered you--pension, disability, travel monies, life insurance, health insurance, etc--so that you should have two amounts to consider, base salary and total package. If you are ABD, you should ask what support they provide for helping you finish, such as a reduced teaching load or freedom from

41

committee assignments. If you are considering several offers, you may be looking at a choice of better pension payments over base salary amounts or a better family leave policy. You may be getting a better deal in the long run with less salary, but with a larger percentage paid to a pension plan or generous time off for children. Consult an accountant or friend with a good business head for advice if you can't make financial sense out of the offers.

If the offer is too low, explain that you had in mind a salary or package more in the range of xxxx. Or you may say you are not willing to come for less than xxx. If they refuse to budge and you want the job, you may ask for a day or two to reconsider or to see if you can work it out. If you are ABD, you may get them to give you some sort of course release in lieu of more salary, which may be less important than time to write.

If you are lucky enough to be contemplating more than one offer, it is fair to use one to up the ante on the other. For example, it is fair to say, "I appreciate your offer and I liked your institution very much. It is at the top of my list of where I want to teach, but xyz university has offered me $xxx more for a similar position. I would be willing to accept your offer if you could match that salary." You may not get an identical match, but something you could live with. Don't make such a demand, though, unless you mean it. In other words, it isn't fair to pump up the offer in one place in order to get another place to offer you more and play them repeatedly off each other.

Before you actually accept an offer officially (and resign from one you have or say no to other offers) be sure to have the details of the offer in writing, especially such things as tenure-track. This is important protection for you if they seem to forget the details of the package, or mistakenly leave something out. It also means they will not be changing their minds, unless the letter carries a qualification about approval from the President or Trustees. Be careful about such qualifications and get final word before taking any other actions.

In addition to salary, rank, and benefits, there are other considerations in deciding what offer you will take. Support for professional development, such as travel funds, secretarial services, teaching assistant or work-study help, a computer set-up, the faculty teaching load, the academic reputation of the institution, faculty morale, family leave policies, and quality of the students are all other things to weigh in deciding. Talk to your advisor, family, and/or friends if you are having difficulty deciding.

Pay attention to your sense of how much the institution wants you. You may never, in your time at the institution, have a better opportunity to negotiate for benefits and other advantages than at the time of your hiring. They may be willing to give you extra things to get you, especially if you have another offer. Do not hesitate to ask for what you want and need if you are fairly confident they want you. You may not have such a bargaining position again unless you receive an offer from somewhere else.

Summary of Chapter Three:
1. Do your homework about salaries.
2. Be willing to negotiate.
3. Use counteroffers carefully.
4. Get the offer in writing.
5. Bargain.

CHAPTER FOUR: FIRST YEAR FACULTY

There is very little in graduate education that prepares a new doctorate for the first year of teaching. Not only do most graduate programs pay little attention to teaching skills, but also many of the strategies that aid survival as a graduate student are counterproductive for new faculty.

Finishing a dissertation often requires hiding away in the library or study and severely limiting the social contacts that might have been important or sustaining at the beginning of graduate school. Becoming a social isolate may not be conducive to one's mental health as a graduate student, but it is often the only way to get a dissertation done. Joining a faculty, on the other hand, is joining a community, and the new faculty member can never afford to forget that. Your new department is not hiring someone only to teach courses and interact with students. They are hiring a colleague, and their feelings about you as a colleague will be of prime importance at every stage of your career: initial evaluation, tenure, promotion, consideration for special grants or leaves, course reductions, etc.

I. Psyching Things Out

Expectations of colleagues vary from institution to institution (and from department to department), and it is partly this uncertainty that makes being a new faculty member so anxiety-producing. Your institution's faculty handbook or personnel manual sets out the official version of your obligations as a faculty member. In fact, the faculty handbook can be considered a legal document that constitutes part of your contract, and you should read it carefully and become thoroughly familiar with it. A number of institutions have begun to rewrite handbooks because of legal pressure, which can make copies of the old handbook scarce. If you do not receive one upon arriving, ask for it. Insist on receiving one, even if it means photocopying a colleague's copy (on the department's budget, not yours). The handbook will not introduce you to the <u>culture</u> of a particular department or institution, however. It will take time to figure out the dynamics of your department and school and the expectations colleagues have of you and each other.

Let's take the department first. Take your time to observe and feel your way in. How much interaction is there among your colleagues and in what context? Do members of the department socialize outside of school? Through what mechanisms, and what is expected in terms of your participation? If dinner parties, for example, are the preferred mode of interaction at your institution, you may have to throw one whether or not they're your "thing." Does interaction revolve around intellectual exchange, personal gossip, college politics, or what? Are there divisions in the department, and, if so, where do they lie? Is one side or the other regarding you as a potential ally or recruit? How do decisions get made? Who has the real power?

It is helpful to check out your perceptions with more experienced colleagues you feel you can trust. One of us spent three years feeling she did not belong in her department because she--quite wrongly--took a very conservative faculty member as speaking for the majority. Finding a community of support is crucial to feeling at home in an institution. At some schools, women's faculty groups can be helpful in extending a welcoming hand and giving you the lay of the land. At smaller institutions, there is often a good deal of interaction among faculty in different departments. Where departments are larger and more isolated, you will have to work harder at seeking out like-minded colleagues in other parts of the school. Sometimes eating in the faculty dining room or at the faculty club can be a good way to meet people. So is going to women's center events, joining interesting committees (see below), or simply making a lunch date with someone you would like to get to know. Colleagues in other departments often have interesting and important perceptions of what is going on in your department.

At the same time it is important to set up a support network, it is also important not to get isolated in a small subgroup whose perceptions may feel immediately simpatico. Try to get to know a range of colleagues and form your own sense of departmental dynamics.

Departments are part of larger institutions, of course, and new faculty will also need to get a sense of the institution of which you are now part. What is the governance structure of the university or college? How much power do faculty have in governance? What are the procedures and personalities involved in getting new courses passed? Are new courses a matter of departmental decision, or are there college-wide procedures? What about tenure and promotion and grievance procedures? Who has the real decision-making power? Are there appeal procedures for different types of grievances? The faculty handbook will give you answers to all these questions, but again there is often a parallel culture existing in and around formal structures and rules. Whether the president listens to committee recommendations, for example, or whether many decisions are made outside formal structures is something only time and more experienced faculty can tell you.

If you are a woman of color it is especially important that you find out the expectations in regard to all faculty concerning their interactions with one another, so that you can determine if there are "special" expectations placed upon you simply because of your minority status. Remember that you have as much right as any other faculty member to set the parameters for interacting and socializing with the other faculty. It is not a part of your professional responsibility to be "the best Black friend" of your White colleagues.

It may seem at times that you cannot win for losing. That is, if you are typically a reserved person, they may perceive your quiet or shy demeanor as hostility and refusal to work with them. If you are more gregarious or assertive they may perceive this as overbearing and aggressive behavior. Being a woman of color and navigating all of the stereotypes of a culturally biased society is not easy. But use your best instincts. It is helpful if you can find some community of support in the university, or someone you can trust in the department. If there is no one at the university you can trust enough to share your experiences, keep close contact with your friends in other institutions. These persons can help you to maintain your sanity. They may become important sounding boards or sources for a reality check when things seem to get strange or strained in your interactions with your colleagues. But most importantly, you do not have to tolerate patronizing or abusive behavior. If you have not already done so, upon arriving at the school find out what recourse you have in addressing this kind of discriminatory treatment. And more importantly, make sure that all expectations of you as a faculty member in relationship to departmental and institutional responsibility are spelled out contractually or in the faculty handbook so that when time comes for tenure you are held accountable only for that to which everyone is held accountable.

Expectations concerning tenure and promotion (topics we will take up in the next chapter) are one important area where formal guidelines and reality often diverge. Many institutions have formal guidelines for tenure that any faculty member can tell you do not reflect the bases on which decisions are made. Some small colleges, for example, really award tenure primarily on the basis of good teaching. Others, however, pay a good deal of lip service to good teaching but actually award tenure on the basis of publications. In many schools, service to the college may be listed as a requirement for tenure along with teaching and publication. But while service may be important in others' perceptions of you as a colleague, it is rarely counted heavily in the tenure decision. These are questions on which faculty who have been around longer can be very helpful. Again, you will want to get the views of a cross-section of colleagues.

II. Making Your Way

Having good information about what is expected does not relieve you of having to make a host of decisions about what kind of colleague you want to be. There is no rule that new faculty have to conform to all expectations. Women are socialized to "be nice," and we often come into a new situation wanting to please everyone. Colleagues don't need to love--or even like--you, however, in order to respect and get along with you.

It is fine to be businesslike and to keep your counsel. It is quite all right to hang back from making commitments of your time and energy until you get the lay of the land. It can also be fine to get involved in faculty politics from the beginning of your appointment. We know of a case where two new faculty members at a rather staid institution made a motion on the floor of the faculty their first year that tenure be abolished. While the motion was regarded with horror by senior faculty, they both got tenure some years later. Sometimes institutions make appointments looking for fresh voices and perspectives. Being a "trouble-maker" in this case will not necessarily count against you, especially if you make trouble intelligently and with good grace!

One decision that faces all new faculty is which and how many committees to sign up for. It is important to get involved in some faculty committees for a number of reasons. They provide a good way of getting to know colleagues in other departments and getting a sense of the workings of the institution. Especially if you are at a school where departments are relatively isolated, committees can be a crucial avenue for meeting other faculty. They also allow you to contribute to and shape college life in areas that are important to you, and they are a way of establishing your value as a colleague. On the other hand, committees can be incredibly time-consuming. They can eat up your life, including the time you need for course preparation as a new teacher, and the time you need to be doing the research that will get you tenure.

It is probably wise not to get involved in any committees your first year, but to devote yourself to teaching and getting to know your school. Then choose committees very slowly and carefully. Do not agree to serve on a committee you are not interested in simply because you feel you ought to say yes. There will always be enough committee work that is actually of interest. You need to look carefully at your own time and figure out how to balance some involvement in college affairs with your teaching and research--and outside--obligations. This is another issue on which more experienced faculty can be helpful. Your chairperson, who will play an important role in seeing you through the tenure process, can sometimes provide good guidance on this question, and may be an important advocate for your doing your own work.

For women of color especially, the important thing is to find out what the committee responsibilities are for faculty members. Do not allow yourself to be overburdened with committee assignments. Remember, it is not your responsibility to be the "minority" voice on the numerous committees in the school. If the faculty is sincere in wanting to have diverse ethnic and gender representation on its various committees, then it should not look to you to fill the void. You should remind the faculty that the best solution to the problem is to have a more representative and diverse faculty.

For any faculty member who takes a first job before finishing the dissertation, warding off committees becomes all the more important. While you are still ill-advised to disappear into the library as if you were a graduate student, finishing the dissertation has to be a top priority until it is done. Expect that colleagues will understand this and help you stick to your guns. Some institutions offer course reductions or special leaves to faculty members working on dissertations, and sometimes you can negotiate such arrangements as part of your initial contract. It is important to discuss this issue before accepting a job. (See "Negotiating an Offer.")

III. Teaching

Even if you come into your first faculty position with considerable teaching experience as a graduate student or adjunct, you will still probably find yourself confronted with a staggering amount of course preparation as you adjust to the needs of your new institution. Until you are able to repeat courses and gain a comfortable sense of your own preparation style, working on courses will take most of your time. For those who do not have teaching experience as graduate students, there are few things more frightening than facing a class for the first time. Perhaps the most important thing to remember is that everyone is nervous. Everyone is worried that she will get through her lecture material in fifteen minutes and have nothing to say. (Sometimes this actually happens, and then you just learn how to lead discussion--fast!) Everyone wonders whether she made a mistake going into teaching, gets down on herself, falls back on teaching the ways she was taught even if she hates them, etc.

Moreover, new women faculty--and especially women of color--often face problems in the classroom not faced by men. Students immediately pick up on whether faculty members are experienced or not, and some will test the authority of women, especially women of color, in a variety of ways. New faculty members may encounter student disruptiveness more appropriate to a high school than a college. They may meet direct challenges to their credentials or authority. Since women faculty members are no more socialized to claim authority than students are to accept women's authority, this can set up a very difficult dynamic. Women committed to non-hierarchical modes of teaching and to "empowering" students often have special trouble claiming the power they need to be effective. It is important to remember that--however you perceive yourself--you have been judged competent to teach your courses and have the right, as well as responsibility, to make the rules that will apply in your classroom.

A sense of your own authority--and style--will come with time, but there is no reason to feel isolated as a new teacher. All your colleagues went through the process of learning how to teach, and this is an excellent topic around which to develop relationships with faculty members with whom you might not have other things in common. This does not mean you need to lay bare your deepest anxieties with every colleague. Except with those you most trust, you can raise questions in terms of general issues and structures rather than your own problems. But however it may feel to you, if you consult with other faculty members about teaching, they are far more likely to come away with a sense of your seriousness as a teacher than with a sense of your incompetence. Ask colleagues what their expectations of students are with regard to readings, exams, etc., and ask how these expectations have changed over time. It is very common for new faculty members to grade over-severely (or in order to be liked, not severely enough), or for new faculty used to thinking in terms of graduate student interests and abilities, to have too-high expectations. Talk with colleagues about how they handle difficult situations or particular topics, how they organize discussions, or deal with the occasional discipline problem. Ask colleagues you respect whether you can sit in on a few of their classes. This is especially helpful if you are teaching a basic course that is taught by several members of the department. If you are having trouble in a particular class, ask a faculty member you respect to sit in and give you feedback. This may feel scary but it can also be very helpful. At some places, "the shortcomings of students today" are a major topic of faculty conversation. While this can get annoying and demoralizing, it can also be helpful in locating and getting distance from your own reactions to students.

Colleagues at other institutions can also be excellent resources for new teachers. Write to or call people who have taught courses you are teaching for the first time. Be aware, however, that more experienced teachers don't always use syllabi as detailed as those you might want to draw up, and a detailed syllabus usually works to your advantage, as well as to students. Your syllabus is your contract with your students. A clear and detailed syllabus tells students what to expect from the course and allows them to decide whether they want to take it. Spelling out course requirements and grading criteria at the beginning of the term also protects you from arguments later.

Often departments that teach a lot of introductory or service courses will expect junior faculty to carry a disproportionate burden of such courses. As a junior faculty member, you should expect to teach introductory or core courses, but you should also ask to teach one or two upper level courses a year in your field. Departments that are fair will distribute electives among all faculty. This is something to discuss in the course of your interview and also to raise with your chairperson your first year. Sometimes you will be replacing a faculty member who has a number of electives in place. Other times you may be hired to teach in a new area. Some schools have complex procedures for introducing new courses into the catalogue, so if there are new subjects you want to teach, you may want to get the process in motion fairly quickly.

IV. Teaching Evaluation Forms

Most institutions use some sort of student evaluation of courses to evaluate your teaching effectiveness. These are often administered by the academic dean's office or by the department. You are given the results after you turn in your grades. While these can be very helpful for assessing your success and troubleshooting particular difficulties in a course, you should read the questions over carefully. If the form does not ask specific enough questions to give you the information you need to evaluate your course, you may also create an evaluation form of your own that can be filled out, brought to your department head or secretary and retrieved after you turn in grades. If you feel your own forms are a better measure of the success of your course, have them added to the personnel file into which the other evaluations are put. These should become part of what is used to assess your eligibility for tenure.

A common problem with institutional evaluation forms is that they are not specific enough to your field, teaching style, or course structure to be helpful to you. Another is that the forms rarely ask what grade the student expects to receive, the student's class standing or overall GPA, or major. Hence, the average score you receive may include the disgruntled "F" student who rarely bothered to show up and was a problem all along. Weak students may also be unable to appreciate the value of your knowledge and the challenges you presented. Finally, people who design the evaluation instruments are not necessarily experts on asking the kinds of questions that yield helpful information. For example, a common question asked is, "the instructor knows her/his subject well." An eighteen year-old first-year student is probably not in a position to judge how well you know your field. Hence, what a student will often actually be evaluating is how authoritative you sound when you present material, which is something that tends to favor typical male gender behavior.

In addition to the general problems with evaluations administered by institutions, there are complications involved in student evaluations of women faculty. The same set of sexist and racist attitudes one finds toward women/women of color in the culture at large will appear in your students. If you are caring and nurturing toward your students, they may conclude you don't know what you are doing because you do not act like a man. On the other hand, if you are authoritative, intellectual, and analytical, they may conclude you are cold-hearted. If you present feminist material, they may decide you hate men or they may argue with you because they refuse to acknowledge your authority. It is the common experience of many of us that students who are taught feminist material by a male professor will quietly accept it as information to be learned in the course. When a woman presents the same material, it is likely she will have the validity of her information questioned or be evaluated as being biased and unfair. This should not dissuade you from presenting feminist material, but you might think carefully about strategies for how to teach it without polarizing your class.

Talk to more experienced feminist colleagues about how they handle such situations. If you are concerned about how this will show up in student evaluations of courses, you are free in your annual self-evaluation, which goes into your personnel file, to discuss reasons you believe you were not fairly evaluated by students in a particular course. One way to defend yourself is to make sure some sort of rebuttal to student feedback appears in your personnel file. If your department head or a colleague is aware of the difficulties you faced, it would be appropriate for her or him also to write a statement that could be put into your file.

V. Departmental Services

Almost all departments provide some backup services for faculty in the form of secretarial help, copy services, student assistants, personal computers, etc. Obviously, the extent of such services is dependent on the wealth and resources of the institution. It is important to find out the kinds of help and services that are available and to make full use of them. At the same time, be aware that if resources are scarce, there is often a pecking order for access to them, and that junior faculty are at the bottom! You may find, especially if secretaries are unused to working for women and people of color, that your syllabi, papers, and letters are the last to be typed. If this happens to you consistently, find out what the rules of accountability are, and don't hesitate to go to a supervisor. Probably the situation will change with time. Remember, however, that treating secretaries with respect and friendliness is more likely to get you help in the long run than pulling rank on them at the outset. Secretaries are invaluable sources of information about the institution and its resource systems. Cultivating a positive, friendly relationship with them will make your life much easier.

VI. Women's Issues

All the issues of finding your way as a new teacher and colleague take on new dimensions if you are the only woman or woman of color in a department, or if there are few women or people of color in your institution. Obviously, in this case, expectations of you as a new colleague cannot be extricated from expectations surrounding the group to which you belong.

It is likely that some people will regard you as a savior and others as a troublesome problem, both for reasons that have nothing to do with you. One of us (a white woman) had colleagues who did not speak to her for years after she became a member of a large all-male department, and it was only after ten years that she realized that many of her male colleagues regularly repaired to the local bar for drinks, and she was never invited. At the same time we may be excluded from informal networks, women, especially women of color, are often under intense pressure to serve on committees so that every committee can have female and/or minority representation. The same goes for moderatorships of student activities. In institutions where there are few women or people of color, women and especially women of color, are often seen by students as saviors, mothers, therapists, defenders against the patriarchy, etc. You may be called on to advise every student group under the sun. While there are important rewards in moderating student activities, just as there can be rewards in committee work, it is also especially important for minority women faculty to guard their time to do their own work so that they do not find themselves in trouble when it comes time for tenure and promotion.

In dealing with all these issues, it is crucial to have a support network. Other faculty can listen to your troubles, provide strategic help, and be a source of mutual support. A group of women faculty at one of our institutions decided we would never agree to join any committee until we had checked it out with two other women who would encourage us to say no! Women faculty who are around for awhile sometimes lose touch with each other because of the burden of class and committee work. Do not hesitate to ask a colleague to sit and talk and have lunch. The contact is often as important for an experienced faculty member as it is for a new one.

VII. Being Out and Maintaining Privacy

Unless you are at a remarkably unfriendly place, your new colleagues will be curious about you as a scholar and a person and may make assumptions about your life or try to get to know you in ways that are not always comfortable. In terms of your personal life, especially if you are unmarried, colleagues may make assumptions about your sexuality and lifestyle that can be false or inappropriate in any number of directions. You are free to reveal as much or as little as you wish, although as a new faculty member, it is wise to parry questions with humor. Lesbians need to weigh the advantages and disadvantages of being out in a new department the same way they would in any new situation. Obviously, being at a seminary or church-related institution in a denomination that has taken a negative stand on gay rights issues raises different problems and considerations from being out at a private or state institution in an area with a gay rights ordinance. Take as much time as you need to evaluate the situation at your school. If you do decide you want to come out, you will also want to think about whether, how, and at what point to bring a same-sex partner to department or institutional social functions and how to introduce her. These issues are not unique to the academic setting, but they can add another level of anxiety to being in a new job.

As we mentioned in the context of the interview section, lesbians who are out in some areas of their lives may not have a choice about whether to come out at a new school. Your new employer will probably have checked you out through the "old boy" or "old girl" networks, and may have been informed about your sexuality through an indiscrete colleague. If you were planning to come out at your new institution anyway, it probably makes most sense to accept with grace the fact that timing is not in your hands. On the other hand, if you do not want to talk about your personal life in your new setting, you might just say something like, "Oh, I didn't know that was public knowledge," and either gently or pointedly change the subject.

Another area in which issues of privacy come up is in relation to students. Like new colleagues, students are also curious about their teachers, especially if the teacher is a member of a group underrepresented at the institution. Different faculty have very different personal styles in relation to issues of self-revelation in and outside the classroom. How much you choose to say about your life is a personal decision, though again one that affects lesbians in a special way. A casual comment about a husband may interest students but isn't going to have any particular reverberations. A similar comment about a same-sex partner has very different implications. Some lesbians are completely closeted with students; others choose to come out in the classroom, especially where their sexuality seems relevant to what they teach; and others come out to students on an individual basis outside the teaching situation. One lesbian faculty member suggested to us that women who want to come out to students might devote some thought as to how to do so subtly or gradually, so that students can hear as much or as little as they want to hear. Someone teaching lesbian material, for example, might say that she is personally very interested in the subject. This would be a cue that some students would pick up on immediately but others might let go by. Or you might have a picture of your partner on your desk, which students can either ask about or ignore.

It is not only in relation to personal issues that new faculty are sometimes put on the spot. You may also find yourself asked to speak on a panel, respond to a paper by another faculty member, or share your work in some public way so that people can get to know you and your views. While this can be very nervous-making, often it is important in allowing colleagues to get to know you and your work, and it can end by helping you make contacts with others who share your interests and who can make you feel more at home. On the other hand, faculty members who have been around for a while sometimes forget the insecurity and vulnerability of new colleagues and make demands that are unfair. We know new faculty members who have been put on the spot responding to very controversial papers, or who are asked to address complex and hotly debated issues at the school. Feel free to politely decline such requests and make it clear that, while you would be happy to do such things in the future, you would like some time to get your bearings first.

VIII. Issues Around Dating

Single faculty members in a new environment who are interested in dating may find themselves confronting difficult personal and ethical questions about relationships with students and colleagues. Some institutions are developing guidelines on these questions. If your school frowns on such relationships, obviously, you would jeopardize your position by entering into one. Regardless of institutional policy, however, we feel that it is ill-advised for faculty members to date students who are in their classes, who are departmental majors, or who are in any kind of direct student/teacher relationship. (See Chapter 8 on Amorous Relationships with Students.) The power imbalance is just too significant and too easily open to abuse. Most women, if they have not themselves been on the wrong end of such a relationship as graduate students, know someone who has. We should be doubly wary then of putting another student in the same position. While we see this ethical principle as applying equally to heterosexual and lesbian relationships, lesbians should be aware that dating students can trigger institutional homophobia, with grave consequences for the faculty member.

Where a faculty member is not in a direct power relationship with a student, the issues become more subtle. Then the power imbalance implicit in their different roles can more easily become simply another issue for negotiation within the relationship. Think hard, however, before getting involved with a student, about the implications of your relationship and where that places you as a new faculty member in relation to students and other members of the faculty.

The same power dynamics present in teacher/student relationships are also present in relationships with colleagues, but with the shoe on the other foot. If a colleague is senior to you and has power over you--and don't forget that senior colleagues, even in very different departments, sit on tenure and promotion and all kinds of grants committees--that colleague should not be in a relationship with you, and you should protect yourself by not dating him/her. Colleagues who are peers present different sorts of issues. If you are considering dating a colleague in your department, consider the effects on other colleagues' perceptions of you. Don't forget that men can get away with things that women cannot. Will the relationship lead to speculations about you that you would rather not invite? Are the two of you likely to be seen as a voting block? Is the relationship likely to affect either of your chances for tenure (more likely yours)? Whether the colleague is in your department or not, what would be the consequences of the relationship ending? Would it be harder for you to do your job? Such calculations may seem cold-blooded, but unless you are looking at a relationship that seems to sweep all other considerations aside, you may as well keep in mind that your work is a major part of your life, and it is important to protect your work environment.

IX. Looking to Move

Sometimes new faculty members are under the impression that if you sign a contract for more than a year, you are obligated to stay at your job for the duration of the contract. Certainly, you should think hard about taking a job you know you will want to leave after a short time. In reality, however, contracts are binding on the university, but they are not binding on the faculty member. If you are unhappy in your job--or if you are offered a better position elsewhere--you are free to leave. Of course, it is only fair to give your department sufficient notice so that they can find someone to replace you, but you are not obligated to inform your department that you would like to move, and in fact it can be unwise to do so until you have another offer. The point at which you tell your chairperson about another possible offer will vary depending on how secure you feel in your position, your sense of how much they want you, etc.

Faculty looking to move should consult the same publications and listings as when you were first seeking a job, but you can also use the contacts you have made since entering the profession. Speak with a few friends at other institutions whose discretion you trust, and see whether you can come up with any openings through the grapevine. Publications are very important as you look to move, so if you are unhappy at your institution, order your priorities to place publication near the top. This should not mean neglecting your obligations to the institution that hired you, but you don't need to keep excessive office hours or get bogged down in committee work if that is not where your commitments lie. Seeking a new job can place you in a delicate situation in that you don't want to alienate your present institution on the hope of moving elsewhere. If you can, talk over strategy with a senior colleague at <u>another</u> institution. When you speak with potential employers, you might want to request that they do not contact anyone at your present institution without checking with you first. Be aware, however, that given the grapevine and informal discussion of applicants among friends, it is quite possible that someone will hear the news anyway. If you are offered a job elsewhere that you want to take, it is not good to leave too much lag time between accepting a new job and moving.

If another institution is courting you and you are unclear about whether you want to move, then other issues emerge. Another offer can be very useful in bargaining with your current institution. It gives you the opportunity to negotiate for increased salary, a course reduction, a student assistant, or whatever else you did not ask for when you first took the job. Using another offer can be a bit like playing chicken, however! Before you try to negotiate, think hard about what you can reasonably ask for and how hard you can push. Also try to be clear about what would make you want to stay. You don't want to be placed in the position of feeling as if you have to move because your demands were not met, when you were not sure you wanted to move in the first place. At the same time, don't forget that there are basically two points at which a faculty member has any leverage in relation to an institution: when she is first hired and when she has an offer from somewhere else. If you know you are wanted, do not let the opportunity pass to make your work life easier or more rewarding.

CHAPTER FIVE: PROMOTION AND TENURE

I.   Tenure

For most academics, tenure is the goal for which one is striving the first six plus years of academic life. In a tight market, getting a tenure-track position is often a plum for which it is worth sacrificing inducements of location, higher salary, or other perks of a one-year or soft money position. Many of the decisions one makes as a junior faculty member--what committees to serve on, requests to agree to, creeps to be nice to, even what scholarship to do--will be made with an eye toward tenure. Almost all institutions have three requirements for tenure: 1) good teaching, 2) scholarship, 3) and service to the college. What constitutes fulfilling these requirements will vary from institution to institution. Keeping tenure requirements in mind is important, but it can also be destructive. It is important not to be obsessed by trying to get tenure.

On the one hand, as we suggested in the last chapter, it is important to get a sense of your institution's real priorities and requirements for tenure during your first year. You will want to find a comfortable balance between doing your own work and being involved in the institution, and you will want to be building a case for yourself from the beginning of your career. We cannot stress strongly enough the importance of keeping full records of all your committee work, moderatorships of student activities, extra advising or work with students, outside lectures, community activities, and, of course, publications. If you have flyers or brochures from outside speaking engagements, thank you notes for lectures you have given or services you have performed, positive book reviews, references to your work in other scholars' writings, keep all these things in a folder. Keep records of new courses taught, courses revised, new teaching techniques you learn or experiment with. If you use feminist or other unorthodox teaching or grading methods, consider writing a statement of your pedagogical philosophy as a rationale for your methods. Do not assume that you will remember every committee you served on or course you introduced when you come to fill out your tenure form years later.

An increasing number of schools are instituting a three year review for junior faculty. This can be nerve-wracking and means more paper work, but it can also be very useful in giving you a sense of where you stand with your department and what kinds of information and materials you will need for the tenure review. At this stage, as your department evaluates the case you and they can make to the administration, colleagues may strongly encourage you to devote yourself to getting out a book or spending more time on committees. If your third year review is oral, write a memo summarizing its main points, send it to the people present to have them confirm its accuracy, and keep the memo in your file. (In fact, this is an important procedure to follow with any oral evaluation of your work.) If you feel a written review misrepresents you, write a response, keep a copy, and have a copy incorporated into your permanent file.

On the other hand, while you will want to try to attend to tenure requirements, you don't want the quest for tenure to shape your life and lead you down paths that are ultimately unsatisfying. If you are not a person who enjoys committees or faculty politics, you do not have to serve on infinite numbers of committees in order to get tenure. Choose one or two activities a year that are genuinely interesting to you. Some women feel that they cannot do feminist scholarship or write on topics related to women until they have tenure. This pressure is doubled for those doing work on minority women's issues. Especially in elite institutions, these are real concerns. We know women who have done significant "mainstream" scholarship who have been penalized because they also did work on women. Some institutions do not consider feminist scholarship "real" scholarship. They have no idea what to do with work that is interdisciplinary. One of us was told at her three year review that her work was too narrow because it was on women! But since it may be excitement about women's and/or minority issues that brought us into the field and that keeps us going, one has to balance such fears and warnings against one's integrity and concerns as a scholar and a person. If the quest for tenure means that you end up writing and thinking about things you are not interested in, it may be better to think about making a move than pursuing tenure at an institution that has no room for your concerns. It is comforting to realize that nonelite institutions are generally much more interested in your being an active scholar than in the content of your scholarship, and there is often much more space at such institutions to pursue nontraditional concerns. This is something that women under siege at elite institutions may want to keep in mind.

The actual tenure review procedure generally has several stages. At some institutions, the review is entirely in-house. You fill out forms describing your teaching, publications, and service, and submit them with supporting documentation (e.g., teaching evaluation forms, reviews of your work, publications) to the appropriate committees. If your chairperson or members of your department have not been sitting in on your classes all along, probably they will evaluate your teaching for the tenure decision. Many departments also want outside letters in support of your application. Often you will be asked to draw up a list of recommended referees. Some departments will pick names from this list, and others will choose some names from the list and some from other sources. Since departments often ask outside referees to do a lot of work on short notice (i.e., read everything you have written within two weeks), it is a good idea to make sure that the people you put down on your list are willing to write for you.

When your dossier is complete, your case will first be reviewed by your department, which will make its recommendation. This stage is crucial in a number of ways. While there certainly are people whose negative departmental recommendations are overturned at higher levels, the support of your department is an important first step on the road to tenure. If a negative departmental recommendation is overturned on a higher level, you then have to live with a department that you know did not want you.

On the other hand, if a positive recommendation is overturned from above, your department can be an important advocate in appeals, grievances, or legal procedures.

Many institutions have university or college-wide tenure committees that consider and pass on departmental recommendations. Some committees will give you the chance to defend yourself, either orally or in writing, against a negative departmental recommendation. Such procedures should be spelled out in the faculty handbook, which you will want to read carefully as you fill out your tenure forms and go through the process. Sometimes deans are members or ex-officio members of the tenure committee, and sometimes your application goes from the committee to the dean, and then to the higher administration. Different institutions have different rules about how much you are told at different stages of the process or what documents you are allowed to see. Find out your institution's rules, and if they seem unfair or problematic, check with your local AAUP chapter or write to the national office. The accrediting agencies of your institution (e.g. ATS) also often have tenure and promotion guidelines.

If you are denied tenure, most institutions have an internal appeals procedure. This should be spelled out in the faculty handbook. If you feel that there was discrimination on the basis of gender, race, ethnicity, religion, or--where this is a protected category--sexual orientation involved in the decision, you should contact the EEOC quickly. Many faculty feel as if they should exhaust all internal appeals procedures before turning to outside agencies. But the statute of limitations on EEOC intervention is sufficiently short that if you wait to contact them, it may be too late. Unfortunately, this can lead you into an adversarial stance, or the appearance of an adversarial stance, vis-a-vis your institution that you wish to avoid, but it is necessary for self-protection.

Summary:

1. Learn your institution's requirements for tenure early on, but try not to be obsessed by them!

2. Keep a careful ongoing record of teaching, scholarship, and service.

3. Make sure you have records in writing of your third year review and all other evaluations. Write memos, if necessary, to create a paper trail.

4. When it comes time to apply for tenure, study your institution's tenure procedures.

5. Choose tenure referees carefully, and make sure they are willing to write for you.

6. If you are denied tenure, take advantage of internal appeals procedures.

7. Go to EEOC quickly if you feel there was discrimination.

II.   Promotion

Most institutions rank faculty members as assistant, associate, and full professors. Promotion brings a higher salary, more prestige, and more responsibility. At most schools, faculty members cannot vote on promotions of those above them in rank. Promotion brings with it more responsibility for evaluating peers, more calls to serve on committees, and often more requests to participate in peer review processes of various sorts (e.g. reading manuscripts, writing letters for colleagues elsewhere) outside your institution.

If you come into an institution with your degree in hand, you will generally be appointed at the rank of assistant professor. At most institutions, promotion to associate professor comes automatically with tenure. Occasionally, faculty members with a strong record of publications will be granted a promotion to associate professor before receiving tenure. This is unusual and is generally a good sign that the tenure decision will be favorable. On the other hand, at some teaching institutions, tenure may be granted on the basis of good teaching, without promotion being automatic. In this case, the faculty member will need to file a separate application for promotion.

Mechanisms and procedures for promotion are generally very similar to those for tenure, and the procedures for making one's case are also very similar. You will need to gather documentation of teaching quality, publications, and service, get outside recommendations or not depending on the institution, and go through a departmental and college review.

Again it is important to keep good records of all activities and to make sure you have written records of any evaluations.

Criteria for promotion may be different from those for tenure, however, and especially at the professor level, may be fairly amorphous. Promotion to full professor generally requires significant achievement, and recognition by one's colleagues outside the institution. While some schools specify a minimum number of years one has to be an associate professor before applying for promotion again, promotion to full professor after that time is never automatic. Some people are promoted fairly quickly, and others remain associate professors throughout their careers.

Perhaps partly because of the amorphousness of criteria for promotion to full professor, this seems to be a point at which many women feel themselves facing discrimination. What constitutes significant achievement? As we discussed in the section on tenure, people who do work in nontraditional fields often find that their work is defined as insignificant from the outset. They are thus called to prove themselves and the validity of their scholarship in ways that would never be demanded of male colleagues. Moreover, because women, and especially women of color are called on to serve on many committees and to moderate student activities, they often do not have as much time to devote to scholarship as colleagues who are pulling less weight in the institution. Committee work and work with students can be intrinsically rewarding, but it is rarely rewarded when it comes time for promotion. Family responsibilities are another important factor that often slow down women's career advancement. Women and men have different career trajectories. Women's work lives often take off--sometimes just begin--as children get older and they have more time for themselves. At the same point in their family lives, however, male colleagues may have their full professorships and begin slowing down.

Two points emerge from these considerations. One, which we discussed in relation to the first year of teaching, is that women are confronted with hard choices for which there are no hard and fast rules. If you feel a sense of responsibility to women at your institution but also want to be promoted, you will probably work harder than a lot of your male peers. You will experience the perpetual "role conflict" that seems to be the lot of the contemporary professional woman, and you sometimes may wonder whether you are doing anything very well. On the other hand, a decision to pursue your own work can also come out of a sense of responsibility to the women in your discipline, and it can be important for students--and administrators--to see women for whom scholarship is a primary commitment. On the other other hand, if you can manage financially, there is nothing wrong with remaining an assistant or associate professor throughout your career and putting your primary energies into activities for which there is little professional reward.

Secondly, however, if it is simply outright discrimination and not more subtle and complex factors that get in the way of promotion, the same avenues of redress are available as in the tenure process. In addition to going through internal review procedures, you can contact the EEOC, and finally get a lawyer and fight your institution in court. It is very important in proving discrimination to be able to show that others in your department or institution were promoted (or given tenure) on the basis of similar or weaker credentials. If the institution has a demonstrable pattern of denying promotion to women, people of color, and/or gays and lesbians, that strengthens your case. Sometimes a faculty women's group can be helpful in gathering data that would show a pattern of discrimination. The affirmative action officer at your school may also track data on tenure and promotion according to gender and racial/ethnic background.

Summary:
1. Learn your institution's criteria for promotion.
2. Keep good documentation of all scholarly activities and all evaluations of your work.
3. Think about your work and life priorities and their relationship to promotion.
4. Know your institution's promotion procedures.
5. If faced with discrimination, take advantage of internal and external review procedures.

CHAPTER SIX: PROFESSIONAL DEVELOPMENT

Once you have accepted an appointment, keeping it depends not only on being able to teach, but also on being an active scholar in your field. Even at teaching-oriented institutions, some level of professional development will be expected. Professional development covers a whole array of items: enhanced teaching effectiveness, publishing, delivering papers, participating in seminars, continuing education, research, travel, and grant writing.

I. Teaching effectiveness.

Some institutions have faculty on staff whose responsibility it is to help you teach writing or oral skills more effectively. Use them as much as you need to. In addition, a number of professional organizations for faculty, such as the General and Liberal Studies Association, the Freshman Year Experience, and the National Women's Studies Association offer conference sections or seminars on teaching effectiveness. Check sources such as the NWSA Newsletter, the Chronicle of Higher Education, and Religious Studies News for announcements of conferences on teaching, new course design, etc. It may be a good use of your travel funds, especially early in your career, to focus on teaching effectiveness.

II. Publishing.

If you are at all able to, you should revise your dissertation for publication or try to publish it in the AAR dissertation series. You may be burned out on it from the graduate school tortures involved, but, since you have already achieved a book-length manuscript, you should try to get some use out of it, if not as a book, at least as essays in journals. You might also pull an essay or two to publish from the dissertation while you work on it as a book. Most publishers are now aware that works on women in religion sell well, so there are a number of places to go if you have such a manuscript. Most university presses, denominational presses, and trade presses seek feminist manuscripts. Your last resort should be a vanity press. This is better than no book at all because a book can be reviewed and get you visibility.

It is not necessarily bad form to send a prospectus of your manuscript to several publishers at one time, as long as they know what is going on. Full length manuscripts are a different story. Sending whole manuscripts out to several publishers is a bit dicey; some editors will refuse to look at something being considered elsewhere. Because editors invest a great deal of time on manuscripts, sending to one at a time is advisable. To lose as little time as possible in the process, ask editors what the timeline is on their decision-making and go with the fastest, working your way through. Another solution is to pick your first choice for publisher, if you have one, and start there. If you have been waiting for awhile for one editor to decide and another press asks to see your work, it is OK to comply, as long as the second press knows you have it out elsewhere. If you are made an offer by either press, you should let the other know. You may find yourself in the nice position of having to weigh counteroffers.

When submitting a prospectus to several editors, send a summary, table of contents, and sample chapters, such as the introduction, a middle chapter, and the conclusion, especially if the manuscript is still in revision stages. When submitting a book to one editor, send the manuscript through the mail with a cover letter asking for a timeline about the decision. If you are still revising, advise the editor of the kinds of changes you are making. The best way to begin negotiations with an editor is to talk to one at a professional association meeting. Most publishers send their religion editors to the AAR. Go to the exhibit hall booths and ask for the editor at each of the presses you want to work with. Ask for time to discuss your project. Be prepared to explain your project briefly to see how interested the editor might be in it. Hold forth with unapologetic enthusiasm. If you don't sound excited about your work, don't expect an editor to be. You might also carry along a summary and sample chapters to give to an editor who expresses interest. Again, ask for a timeline about decision making.

Additional factors in selecting a publisher, if you have no first choice in mind, are important to consider. Does the publisher seem to do a good job of promotion and advertising of authors' works? Does the press have a good distributor (if you've had trouble ordering for a press, don't use it yourself!)? Do you like the quality of their editing? Do they publish authors you like? Would it be to your advantage to publish with the press associated with your religious group? Do you think you will enjoy working with the editor? Ask editors what books they have worked on and talk to the authors about their experiences with the editor, if you are uncertain.

There are somewhat standard amounts trade publishers offer for contracts on first books, since you are an untried author. University presses, Scholars Press, and some denominational presses offer no advances. Don't expect to get rich on your first book unless it is on a very hot topic in high demand. If you know someone who has recently published, ask them what they were offered. The standard trade press offer includes an advance of somewhere between $1,000 to $2,500 (as of 1990) plus a royalty on a certain percentage after a minimum number of sales. Since your advance comes out of royalties, look closely at the royalties percentages, including the paperback rights and translation rights. If you are uncertain about the contract you are offered, ask another scholar who has published and has some experience with contracts to look it over. In addition to money, you should look for how much editorial control you will have over things like the title, cover, and text.

Most contracts stipulate that your publisher will have first access to your next book. This may be great if you like your publisher. On the other hand, if your first experience is unpleasant, this clause is usually not a serious problem. Some authors ask the publisher to strike the clause or you may strike it before you sign. You can always refuse their offer, if you submit your next manuscript to them. Authors sometimes ignore this clause of their contract. You might get sued by a publisher, but it is hardly worth it to them to sue you or incur your ill will unless a lot of money is involved. Editors like to curry the favor of promising new authors, not make them angry.

In negotiating a contract, you should try to maintain as much control over the project as possible. Even if you like and trust your editor, which is an ideal situation, you may find yourself stuck with a title you hate or with an embarrassing cover. At least try to maintain veto power over titles and covers.

Other than books, the publishing that gains points toward tenure are serious, scholarly essays. In some fields, blindly refereed articles are the only ones taken seriously. This seems less so in many areas of religion, in which an essay in a good anthology or in any reputable journal is highly regarded. Hence, if you are invited to submit to an anthology or journal, do so. If you publish feminist material, there are still few journals that wholeheartedly accept such work. Some journals, such as Encounter, Religion in Intellectual Life, Cross Currents, and Theology Today have had special issues on feminist subjects and periodically publish such material, so contemplate submitting work there. A further problem with publishing work on women and religion is that beyond The Journal of Feminist Studies in Religion, feminist journals such as Signs or Feminist Studies tend to accept only essays that are historical or social scientific. Hypatia accepts philosophical ones. If you know an editor at a journal, write a letter of inquiry to see if they would be interested in your work. When submitting, follow the formatting guidelines specific to each journal (often published somewhere in each edition) and enclose a cover letter introducing yourself and your work briefly. Often your best bet for publishing an essay is an anthology. You can, of course, consider putting together an anthology of your own in consultation with a publisher.

III. Papers and conferences.

Many institutions will not pay your way to a professional meeting unless you are giving a paper, or you may get more funding help if you do. In any case, it is important early in your career to give papers so that you become known by your colleagues in the field. It is best to start attending meetings like the AAR/SBL while you are still a graduate student, especially the regional meetings, which are usually much less expensive. Get to know the section chairs of your areas of interest at the regional level and discuss ways for you to submit paper proposals. It also doesn't hurt to get to know regional officers and to volunteer to chair a section. Presenting your first paper at a regional AAR/SBL is a good idea if the thought of the national meeting intimidates you. The regional meetings are usually much smaller and are more informal in tone. You will also have a chance to get to know other women scholars in your region and develop networks.

At the national AAR/SBL, you should attend your first meeting without having to give a major paper, if that is at all possible. You will be able to get a sense of the meeting without huge stress or an elevated anxiety level and focus your attention on meeting people and getting acquainted with the various sections. It also helps to attend with a friend so you can cover more territory and keep each other company at events. Attending the annual meeting alone, especially if you are new and don't know many people, can be an alienating, exhausting and harrowing experience. The meeting has gotten huge and increasingly impersonal and fragmented. The Women's Caucus: Religious Studies meetings and reception are a good place to meet other women in the field. Even if you know people, unless you make an arrangement to meet them before you come, you cannot count on running into or finding them.

Come to the annual meeting with some idea of papers you could deliver the following year. Then make an effort to attend the business session of sections that fit with your scholarly interests and make program suggestions that would open avenues for your work. Failing in that, introduce yourself to section chairs and ask if your work would be appropriate. When the call for papers appears for the next annual meeting, consider sending out proposals to two sections, but no more, which will increase your odds somewhat of getting something accepted.

IV. Other miscellaneous items.

Institutions appreciate faculty who are able to bring in outside funds. You should practice grant writing skills to get fellowships or grants for research, travel, additional education, or conferences. Most institutions also have special internal funds for such things, but it doesn't hurt to look outside at the same time. Getting a Fulbright, NEH grant, or other such award, even if it might mean taking a semester's or year's leave of absence, will usually be positively regarded because it adds to the visibility and prestige of the institution. The academic dean's office usually has information about applications and deadlines.

However you can do it, find the funds to keep your research going and avail yourself of travel or other professional development opportunities whenever possible.

CHAPTER SEVEN: MATERNITY AND CHILD CARE

Different women choose to bear children at different times, according to their particular personal, professional, and biological circumstances. Some begin the process while in their early twenties, during or just after college. At some later point, they go on to doctoral studies, and enter the workforce with their family already established. Others postpone childbearing until they have secured tenure; these women are thus often in their late thirties or early forties when they first become pregnant. But for many new Ph.D.s, the years of greatest professional vulnerability--establishing a professional self, developing syllabi, learning to teach, creating a tenure dossier--coincide directly with the most desirable years for starting a family.

I.   The Interview

If children are on your horizon, find out what you can about a potential employer's maternity leave policy when investigating faculty benefits. Often the information will not be presented clearly in the faculty handbook which you should receive; moreover, the faculty interviewing you, if they themselves have not had to know, will have little idea of the institution's policies. You may feel hesitant about inquiring directly, and for good reason. Pregnancy is doubly suspect: first, because it is an exclusively female condition; second, because it may be perceived as a choice which compromises one's expected total dedication to the academy: True Professionals Don't Get Pregnant. Some potential colleagues may view your inquiry as the first step toward your taking undue advantage of institutional benefits, an excuse to delay the tenure decision or decrease your number of contact hours. Others may conclude that your primary interests are in the home rather than in the academy.

How, then, should you proceed? First, get what information you can from the faculty handbook and the literature on benefits. Second, ask your contact person on campus to include in your on-site interview a meeting with the Affirmative Action or the Benefits officer. The fact that these people will be outside your prospective department will facilitate frank discussion. Third, have your contact person also arrange for you to meet with other women--including those untenured--on the faculty.

Specifically request to meet with faculty who have had children while in the institution's employ. A "Women's Concerns Committee" may exist on your campus, and would be a likely source for identifying appropriate faculty. Fourth, if you have free time to look around campus during your visit and you spot a pregnant woman, do not hesitate to ask her (a) if she is indeed faculty herself and (b) if so, what sort of arrangements she made with the institution. Finally, while you should speak with your departmental chairperson in some detail about such matters as course load, administrative responsibilities, office hours, etc., you should not expect him or her to be familiar with the institution's current maternity policy. Count on having to research the issue yourself.

If your position is to be part-time or contractual rather than tenure-track, double check all information you receive. Benefits that extend to full-time faculty may not apply to all, or may apply only in part to you. Some institutions are willing to create special packages for non-tenured or tenure-track appointees: it may not hurt to ask. If you are the partner of a pregnant woman or you are planning on adopting, these same guidelines, mutatis mutandis, apply.

II. Benefits systems

For those institutions lacking set maternity benefits, the most reliable information you receive is often by word of mouth. This is so because, as with no other personnel-related issue, not only do maternity policies vary widely from institution to institution but also, within the institution, access to policy information varies widely. At one extreme stand those institutions that automatically extend comprehensive maternity benefits to full-time faculty (e.g., one quarter or semester off at full pay; insurance coverage; cessation of the tenure clock during maternity leave); at the other, those that offer no benefits at all, consequently leaving the faculty with the option either of no leave or leave without pay. Occupying the middle ground are those institutions that decide benefits on a case-by-case basis.

The third system usually treats pregnancy and maternity leave, for the purposes of insurance and health benefits, as a temporary disability. In this case, released time following childbirth is often determined not by the academic calendar but by some hypothetical medical one, with leave permitted for six to eight weeks. Such a system usually construes maternity leave for faculty as it would for full-time staff. However, while staff can be replaced by temporary workers, faculty usually cannot. Further, non-academic time increments wreak havoc with semester-long courses (how can you miss six to eight weeks of a semester, trimester, or quarter?). The case-by-case system indicates both the lack of clarity surrounding maternity policies for academics and an instinctive institutional parsimony regarding pregnant faculty.

But do not despair. According to the 1978 Federal Pregnancy Disability Amendment to Title 7 of the 1964 Civil Rights Act, institutions are required to extend to pregnant full-time faculty the same coverage accorded to other faculty for "comparable" medical situations: pregnancy, childbirth, and recovery must, at the least, be covered as "physical disability" would. Those institutions lacking a systematic disability policy, however, are free to consider pregnancy etc. on a case-by-case basis. An official letter from your physician reviewing your medical condition and suggesting an appropriate recovery period (caesareans, for example, require more recovery time than vaginal delivery; the medical analogue is abdominal surgery, not vaginal childbirth) will help your dean, provost, or chairperson to project the appropriate amount of leave.

If you are asked your opinion on how much released time you anticipate needing, please:

A.   Resist the temptation to be heroic. If you are back in the classroom too soon, you suffer, your students suffer, and no one will be cheering you from the sidelines.

B.   Resist as well the feelings of guilt that may accompany your decision to remain home, refuse additional committee work, delay submission of written work, etc. Pregnancy and parenting will unavoidably take time from academic pursuits.

C.   Be realistic. Recovery often takes longer than you think. To survive the early years of full-time teaching, you will have acquired excellent reality-denial skills ("I'm not that tired. I can do this. What's one more committee/book review/panel response/set of papers...?"). Repress them. Recovery from pregnancy and childbirth is, for most women, different in kind from managing with "normal" sleep deprivation and stress.

III.   Pregnancy

If you have decided to become pregnant, bear several things in mind. For most women, the first trimester is a period of enormous fatigue. If you are untenured and can barely manage to do what you have to do putting in 16-hour days, realize that, at least for the first trimester, the proportions of waking to sleeping hours will virtually reverse and that, for the eight or so hours a day you do manage to stay awake, you may very well be moving in a hormonal fog, able to talk and to teach but not effectively research or write. A colleague has dubbed this condition "Milk on the brain."

Some women anticipate these circumstances by attempting to become pregnant late in spring or early summer, when school is not in session. However, this schedule will mean that delivery and recovery time will likely fall in the middle of the spring semester. Should you wish to plan either the onset of pregnancy or delivery for the summer months, speak with your OB-GYN. But remember: becoming pregnant is not within your conscious control. It can happen immediately; it can take months or even years. You should therefore be as prepared as you can for any eventuality.

Should you encounter problems with conception, your institution's insurance package may pay for fertility counseling or treatments. If your school offers more than one insurance package (e.g., various HMOs, Blue Cross/Blue Shield), register with the policy that will provide the services you need. Other faculty may have valuable information and advice about fertility specialists, hormonal treatments, and surgical procedures; still others, on adoption agencies. Ask.

One important factor over which you have control is your work. Particularly if you have your children while you are untenured, it is in your own interest to have syllabi compiled and written work completed and submitted for publication. Few things better belie the aura of pregnancy-induced 'unprofessionalism' than a publication or two right around delivery time (and the length of gestation, both with a publisher and with a baby, is about the same).

Because of the chance of spontaneous miscarriage, and for some, the decision to terminate a pregnancy because of problematic AFP, CVS, or amniocentesis reports, many women prefer to wait past the initial twelve-to-fourteen week period before publicizing their pregnancy. If you experience incapacitating distress during early pregnancy, however, you should probably confide in your chair or dean or provost. If your department is planning courses for the semester in which you plan to take maternity leave, you should also seriously consider confiding in your chairperson early on. Most administrators will understand and respect your concerns about confidentiality, and they will likely appreciate being informed of your potential absence with as much lead time as possible.

IV. Coping

A. Working While Pregnant

Have enough of your work under control before you get pregnant so that, once you are, as many things as possible can continue without your having to undertake new tasks. Be ruthless in declining requests to serve on more committees than those to which you have already been assigned, and ease out of as many extraneous obligations as you can. You may have to. For most women, sleep becomes a major occupation in the first trimester, and you will simply not have enough time to sleep and teach if you also have innumerable other responsibilities. The second trimester of pregnancy is usually, for most women, much easier and less fatiguing.

Nausea--unbelievable, debilitating, non-negotiable nausea--is also a frequent fact of pregnancy. Euphemistically called "morning sickness," this condition can persist throughout the day, invade only in the afternoon, and/or continue long past the first trimester. Others experience periods of dizziness or even fainting: these soap-opera symptoms of pregnancy correspond to Real Life. You might carry saltines or some other dry cracker with you. You might sit or lie down or in general do, whenever possible and socially seemly, whatever affords some semblance of relief. But what you definitely can do is:

-- Arrange in advance not to teach early morning classes. By mid-morning, you will most likely be able to function better.
-- Arrange for lecture halls to have a stool by the lectern so that you can sit, if you need to, while teaching.
-- Tell your class that you are pregnant. Students will be less alarmed if you grow suddenly faint and need to pause. One assistant professor of biblical studies, upon alerting her class on Christian origins to her problems with dizziness, was asked by a student if she had recently conversed with an archangel. "No," she replied, "and I'm not a virgin either." The group over-all responded with increased consideration--helping carry materials to class, moving audio-visual equipment, voluntarily restricting non-office hour contact.

While some institutions have no dress code, either written or unwritten, others prefer their faculty attired in a "professional" manner. Most affordable maternity clothes unpleasantly recall antimacassars or Laura Ashley wallpaper; non-ruffled, non-pastel maternity clothes are priced for those who work in law firms.

Cultivate lawyer friends and borrow clothes from them; seek out stores that sell clothes second hand. Some effort to look as you normally do will subtly reassure colleagues and students that you are, indeed, still you. Similarly, you should keep a change of clothes in your office for both pre-partum symptoms (e.g., excess sweating in the latter months of pregnancy, sensitivity to heat or cold, vomiting) and post-partum problems (from shoulders covered with baby's lunch to milk stains down the front of your blouse. Nobody said this process was elegant.)

If you and your fetus are both in good health, and you, your due date, and the academic calendar are reasonably in sync, there is no reason not to work until you deliver. Indeed, this can be beneficial. Working to the end of term (sic) can mitigate the somatic equivalent of cabin fever. True, lecturing while trapped inside 25-to-50 extra pounds is not exactly an out-of-body experience, but it does keep you from spending all your time wondering when It will be over.

Simply by being there, you present a valuable message to your students and colleagues: Women are definitely part of the workforce, and they need not choose between a family and career (more on this below). You may even find that you enjoy a pleasant sense of invulnerability: extremely pregnant women are difficult to argue with--about anything. If you do work to your due date, be sure that at least one person in your department knows how to contact your labor coach (if you have one) and what to do when you go into labor. You might also alert a sympathetic student, should you go into labor during class.

B.   Complications

So far, this information has been based on the supposition that you and your child are both healthy. If you have experienced difficulties beyond the normal ones of pregnancy and delivery (confined bed rest, caesarian, rupture), alert your departmental chairperson and dean or provost as soon as possible if you do not think your previously negotiated leave time will suffice. (Again, a letter from your physician will help make your case.) If your child will require extra care, extended hospital stay, surgery, etc., you should also inform the appropriate institutional personnel.

Extreme emotional lability and/or depression frequently follow childbirth. See your doctor at once. Post-partum depression, though temporary, is a serious condition: do not call on those denial techniques, mentioned above, and assume that you can pull yourself out simply by plunging back into your academic work. Seek medical help. Your insurance package will probably pay for the medications and counseling involved.

C.   Child Care Arrangements

By the beginning of the third trimester, you should make child care arrangements. Good child care arrangements are the difference between a healthy, happy child in a healthy, happy family and a short route to the inner circle of hell.

Treat arranging for child care as you would a part-time job. Investigate options even while you are conceiving of conceiving. Often the best facilities have long waiting lists. During the first post-partum months, when you are still on maternity leave, you can ease into child care arrangements. Especially if you are breast-feeding, you and your child will be all but physically connected. Yet it can help both of you to get a break from each other and you can check for glitches in your child care and still have time to change. Keep in mind, however, that for your child, changing child care people frequently is the emotional equivalent to coming home to a different spouse every night. The formation of an emotional bond with the child care personnel and a consistency of location lead to happy children. Happy children usually lead to happy, productive academic mothers.

It is well to give some thought not only to your individual circumstance in searching for child care, but also to the larger social and political climate that shapes women's lives in the United States. Because we all live in a society that does not value its children and that deems certain races and classes expendable, it is inevitable that many racial/ethnic minority women are in child care work and that they are grossly underpaid. As an academic woman, even if you are in a two-income family (which is not by any means the norm), you do not have a lot of discretionary income whence must come the additional expense of child care. The trajectory of exploitation that has its start in American slavery and in the exploitation of immigrant women can pass through your own home.

How do we concretely manage our lives as mothers who work outside the home and not participate in the further exploitation of women? Critical as a starting point is the recognition that the care of children is honorable work. Low pay, inadequate benefits, unpaid vacations, long hours, lack of job security--these are its exploitative dimensions. Therefore, child care arrangements must be made that take advantage of opportunities for cooperative endeavor to provide decent working conditions for those who provide it.

Some institutions provide childcare for faculty and graduate students. Make inquiries about whether workers do receive a living wage and benefits. Cooperative childcare is financially attractive and often cooperatives are run by people who have some sense of larger social and political issues. For wife/husband families, this is the major political negotiation that needs to go on: fathers need to provide half the child care. Lesbian couples often have far less trouble negotiating this one. But it is simply true that next to every successful working mother usually stands a significant other who does a lot of the work. Single mothers have found it critical to band together and try to provide this kind of support for one another.

Creative financing of quality childcare is a good strategy. Some institutions offer benefit bank vouchers. While these can be attractive, some programs force a choice between child care and health care. If you do have a benefit bank, inquire about contributing part of your salary into the program so that you can pay for child care with untaxed dollars.

Some institutions subscribe to sitter services; some faculty have found helpful a series of student sitters. These arrangements have several drawbacks. Lack of consistency is suboptimal. And now is the time to pay attention to every parent's nightmare, but one you must confront and strategize against: child sexual abuse. Childcare attracts pedophiles. This is a fact of life. New guidelines developed by the Boy Scouts of America, who have tried to deal forthrightly with the amount of pedophilia in their organization, require a six month waiting period until a volunteer can have sole contact with a child.

For one of us, a first pediatrician was a woman who had five children. What this woman didn't know about child care was not worth knowing. She recommended that sitters be interviewed, references checked, and a physical examination be given by a reputable physician (and the results paid for and sent directly to the employers). Problems such as AIDS and other infectious diseases, high blood pressure, substance abuse, etc. can be picked up in such a procedure. Treat the employment with a high degree of professionalism. You will never make a more important decision.

D.   Re-entry

You have weathered morning sickness. You have survived the delicate negotiations with your department and your dean about maternity leave. You have taught while blind with fatigue and green with nausea. You may even have given birth to a publication or two. You have watched as your body changed shapes in ways you would not have imagined possible, maintained your composure while subject to hormonal tsunami (tidal waves) and tedious jokes about dirigibles and the Queen Mary. One way or the other, you delivered your baby.

The easy part is now over.

If you had little time for yourself before, you will have less now. You may find yourself achieving new heights of effectiveness, actually getting work done when you sit down to do it, because your work hours will be so circumscribed. You may even develop the ability to touch type one-handed, as the other is now occupied holding a sleeping or nursing child. Especially if your baby is in group childcare outside your home, you will be exposed to the usual soup of germs all children live in, and thus will be introduced to ear infections, fevers, and various intestinal unpleasantries. Unpredictably broken nights, the demands of either nursing or preparing bottles at 2:00 a.m., and the delights of unexpected effluvia erupting from your precious bundle will be added to your list of life experiences. You are exhausted; you are perpetually sticky; you are stressed; you are happy. Go figure.

Some women choose--for lack of other options, for financial reasons, or to continue nursing--to keep the child in the office once back at work. Before you move the playpen next to your desk, speak first with your chairperson and neighboring colleagues: you should not present them with a new office mate without some warning. Assure them that the baby is quiet and that, if not, you will make other arrangements. If your baby is fretful or colicky, be fair: your colleagues should not have to try to work in conditions that you yourself can scarcely tolerate.

Have plastic bags readily available for soiled diapers: do not allow your office to smell like a nursery. Should you decide to use student sitters, having the child in your office may prove to be a major convenience for everybody. The sitter may retrieve the child there, proceed to the park or the dorm for a few hours, and return when it's time for nursing.

V.   Other models

The above discussion presupposed the situation of a pre-tenured woman aged somewhere in her late twenties or early thirties. Pregnancy while still junior can delay your tenure decision not only indirectly (i.e., because of delays preparing publishable material) but also directly: often, institutions permit a woman to slow down the tenure clock for a semester or a year for each maternity leave. (Some institutions extend this consideration for adoptive parents, too.) This delay has the benefit of relieving some pressure, though it also protracts the pressured period.

Some women choose to secure tenure before having their babies. The obvious advantage of this decision is professional security: your publications and presence are known in your field; temporary absence feels less like disappearance. The disadvantage is physical. The younger you are, the less intense the strains of pregnancy. A pregnancy at forty is, in this simple sense, more work than a pregnancy earlier. In an equally simple sense, however, physical strain may be preferable to the stress of starting a family when still professionally vulnerable. You should note, however, that fertility decreases dramatically after age 35, while the incidence of Down's syndrome and other fetal abnormalities probably increases.

Pregnancy at a relatively late stage may affect your career in a different way. Should you wish to move into a position of administrative authority, chairing a department, becoming a dean or provost to serving on a national committee--a new baby may very well impede you precisely at the time when you are ready and perhaps even eager for new responsibilities.

VI. Closing Statement

Most men do not have these problems. Most men need not feel, to prove their professional seriousness to themselves and others, that they must choose between a career and a family. Starting a family, especially while untenured, will occasion fatigue, stress, and anxiety in male faculty too; but invariably the heavier burden, both professional and physical, falls on women.

Within the next twenty years an increasingly significant proportion of Ph.D.s in the humanities will be women--in some fields, they are already a majority. Human biology cannot change to accommodate this shift in academic demography. Health insurance, benefits packages, and tenure clocks, however, can. That much, at least in part, is up to us.

You may choose to ask your institution to establish a maternity policy or modify an existing one. If you do, be prepared to be asked to obtain data from comparable institutions, to solicit information on finances and projected start-up costs, to determine how faculty benefits will achieve parity with staff, to organize infant, toddler, and pre-school care, etc.

This is a huge undertaking. Should you decide to assume the task, do not do it alone. Ask that a committee be formed, composed of staff and faculty, junior and senior, and request a budget for student or secretarial support. Gathering information is expensive, tedious, and time-consuming, and you will have your own research and work to attend to.

One Last Word: Guilt

If you have finished reading this chapter and still intend to have children, you will become familiar with the constant companion of every mother who works outside the home: Guilt. Am I doing enough for my child? Is my work suffering? Is my child suffering?

Take a deep breath and relax. Chances are that, if you like what you do and you feel that you contribute to work you think is important, you will be a better person to be around. Children can learn a lot in quality childcare: how to get along with kids their own age, how to trust others, especially other adults, how to begin to learn what and how to do for themselves. Even if you can't bake cookies with them as often as you think they might like, even though you miss a midday school recital and forget to buy their friend's birthday present on time, even though, as the years roll by, you will hate yourself each time you accidentally or with forethought miss one of your child's activities, remember: she or he will probably, despite this, grow up to be a decent human being.

Ultimately, remember this: There is no way to be a perfect mother; but there are millions of ways to be a good mother. You will be.

CHAPTER EIGHT: HANDLING DIFFICULT SITUATIONS

This last chapter addresses some of the most difficult and stressful circumstances you may encounter in an academic career. Should you encounter any, the choices you make about what to do may have a long-term impact on your career. We discuss these issues because, if you are faced with these circumstances, it is helpful to have thought about them ahead of time. We hope you are lucky enough to avoid at least some of these problems.

In addition to sexual harassment there is outright discrimination in hiring, promotion and other areas as well as something the EEOC calls "Discrimination on account of sex." This consists of expectations which are sex specific. For example, one of us was expected to attend to sick faculty colleagues because she was female and "women are supposed to understand such things." Such an expectation was clearly determined by her sex. Sometimes it is visible in lower access to secretarial services because "women know how to type." Often women are assigned to the department hospitality (sunshine) committee or given all assignments related to gender issues. Whatever the negative treatment you receive, if you decide to take formal action, be sure to determine the accurate category for your complaint, for example sexual harassment vs. discrimination on account of sex. Become familiar with the definitions your institution uses (they should be spelled out in a faculty handbook).

I.   Sexual Harassment

Virtually every woman in a seminary or university at some point will experience harassment and/or be a victim of sexual misconduct. Sexual harassment is not an inconvenience; it changes lives. It can be frightening, intimidating, embarrassing, and highly stressful. It includes but is not limited to the following: sexist remarks or behavior, insults, lewd, obscene or suggestive remarks or conduct, displays of degrading sexual images, unwanted touching, inappropriate or repeated social invitations following previous refusals, requests for sexual favors with or without implied reward or punishment, and, of course, attempted or completed assault.

Most of us have been inured in our lifetimes to innuendo, whispered comments, jokes, whistles, honking, winks and grimaces. When these become an everyday fact of life in the workplace it becomes harder to dismiss them as the behaviors of ignorance. The people we work with, after all, are supposed to be able to recognize our credentials and talents. It often comes as a shock to new graduate students to find that the doctorate has made little difference in how their sexuality is viewed by male colleagues.

Frequently it comes as a shock to men to learn that most professional academic women are not flattered by this behavior. The problem is exacerbated by the fact that there are some women who tolerate it with humor or appear to "play the game." Since we are all products of our culture, both sexual harassment and the various reactions to it must be carefully examined in order to create effective strategies for handling it. Attempts to dismiss or overlook sexual harassment may leave a woman feeling more powerless than the harassment itself. The following strategies are suggestions for those who have decided to take action against it.

A.   Informal Strategies for Facing Sexual Harassment

The formal processes surrounding sexual harassment complaints may take many weeks to conclude. In the meantime, some harassers will continue their activities even as you await formal justice. Whether or not you consider bringing formal charges against a harasser, it is to your benefit to have planned strategies for dealing informally with sexual harassment. In the event you do not file a formal grievance, which happens in the minority of cases, your development of strategies for handling harassment directly, at the time it occurs, will be important to maintaining your own mental health. The following suggestions for coping with harassment are gleaned from the oral tradition of many who contributed to this manual.

Before choosing a strategy, it is helpful to identify the kind of harasser you are confronting. Just as there are several types of rapists who assault their victims for different reasons, sexual harassers vary in their motivations and in their methods. While you may not be able to identify the type of harasser exactly, having a general idea of the problem you are confronting can enhance your effectiveness.

Some harassers enjoy the surge of power and control that comes from a woman's reaction to their harassing. They are sometimes so accustomed to power that they do not recognize their behavior as wrong. Passive avoidance, meekness, or apologetic behavior will mark you as an easy victim and encourage aggression. All semblances of acquiescence or submission will make you inviting prey. With this type, be sure you continue to attend committee meetings and attend to your work in a business-like manner even when the harasser is present. Confront his/her behavior directly and firmly. "I do not find this behavior humorous. I find it offensive, disconcerting, and distracting from my work. Do not do it again." Or, "Your behavior (joking/language/inappropriate touching) creates difficult working conditions for me. Please do not do it in my presence." Or, "I would very much appreciate being treated as an equal colleague. We have no other special relationship to one another." Whatever you say, look the harasser in the eye; say your statement in a calm, firm, even tone of voice; and repeat it several times if it is shrugged off or dismissed. (Practice with a friend role-playing the harasser, if you think that will help you do it.) You are not required to explain yourself. If the harasser demands to know why the behavior in question bothers you, you should not get yourself trapped into the subordinated position of having to justify yourself to someone who harasses you. If an explanation is asked for, simply repeat your statement. You might add, "I do not care to explain myself to you. I simply ask you to stop the behavior." Remember that power is a booster of self-confidence for this type of harasser, so he/she may try to up the ante by escalating the behavior first. Remain calm (anger, tears, or hysteria will be a sign the behavior "got" to you).[1] Say the same firm statement over. If the behavior does not stop after several attempts, you may add a statement such as "I have repeatedly asked you to stop this behavior. You should know that it constitutes the legal definition of sexual harassment (be sure you know the state or institution's definitions when you say this), and, since you have refused to cease at my request, I will be filing a formal complaint against you (or will file a complaint the next time you harass me)." (Do not say this unless you mean it.) When you speak, do not smile, joke, or give any impression that you could be dissuaded from your conviction. Attempts to seem nice will feed into cultural stereotypes that nice girls say no when they mean yes. If the behavior does not stop, you may also approach your department chair, divisional dean, or a senior colleague, whom you trust, to mediate for you informally. You should ask this person to talk to the harasser on your behalf. Whatever means you take, **keep written records of every incident, conversation, and action you take**, in case you have to file a formal complaint.

Power harassers vary from the relatively ignorant types, who have learned their behavior to cope with their uncomfortableness with relating to women as equals, to the sinister types, who thrive on intimidating others and are sometimes capable of doing you physical harm. You may be endangering your personal well-being

---

[1]For a helpful book on managing anger and developing effective, assertive techniques for coping with highly charged emotional situations, see Harriett Lerner's The Dance of Anger (New York: Harper & Row, 1986).

if you treat their behavior lightly and laugh it off or attempt to ignore it. Act firmly and forcefully to make your wishes known.

The other end of the spectrum from power harassers are those who use a sense of victimization to manipulate others. These types lack clear, respectful personal boundaries and expect others to meet their needs. They will often select you if you seem accessible, sympathetic, and sexually vulnerable. They may begin by telling you their personal problems, a form of self-disclosure that leads eventually to their sharing of their sexual frustration. The technique is to lure you into a voluntary affair. If you try to withdraw, they may retaliate with hostility or attempt to sabotage your work and relationships with other colleagues. If a new colleague of yours begins to share intimate personal information with you in great confidence, especially in relation to intimate personal relationships, you should establish clear boundaries. As soon as the harasser begins to share personal information, you might say something like, "I am sure this problem causes you great personal pain, but this is information that should be shared with a close personal friend or therapist. I would rather not get involved and would prefer to keep our relationship a collegial one." Then change the subject to one related to business. Remember that this type of harasser is experienced at emotional manipulation and will select victims who seem willing to take care of them, who are nice and accommodating, and who appear eager to accept confidences. If you have a colleague who seems overly friendly, who is inordinately helpful, or who seems to want your company a great deal, avoid one-on-one appointments with the person. If they ask you to lunch, invite another colleague along and say, "I have invited X along. I thought it would be nice to have a threesome." Or, "I have also wanted to get to know X, so I have invited her/him along. I hope that is OK." If it is not, find a reason to cancel (children or cats can fall suddenly ill, you can develop a headache, or you can forget you had planned a lecture for your 1:00 class and need to work over lunch, etc.) or make sure you go to a very public place--like the faculty club or a place used by other colleagues. If you find yourself inadvertently alone with him/her, do not linger, but move on. If none of the above works to discourage the harasser, you may confront him/her directly with a clear statement such as, "The sharing of inappropriate sexual information constitutes lewd behavior. I have clearly indicated that I do not want to hear such conversation from you. If you continue to seek me out, I will file a formal complaint of sexual harassment against you."

Keep in mind that regardless of the type of harasser, your informal responses may trigger escalation and retaliation, and a formal complaint may leave you open to reprisal and create a poor reputation. One way to protect yourself is to be sure you have discussed the problem informally with an administrator or senior colleague who will help protect you if retaliation occurs. This is someone who should be able to put a credible letter in your tenure file and who can be your support or advocate should formal proceedings become necessary. While confronting sexual harassment can have serious negative consequences, avoiding confronting it can also affect your health, job satisfaction, and relationships with your colleagues.

Whatever else you do, do not blame yourself. About 85% of all women in a variety of studies report sexual harassment in the workplace. Women experience harassment regardless of age, race, affectional orientation, marital status, class, or appearance. Most women who report harassment also remain in their jobs out of necessity. You are not encouraging harassment or being complicitous by continuing your position! Refuse self-blaming and seek out a feminist support system to reduce the painful effects of this sexist scourge.

B.   Formal Grievance Processes

The decision about whether, when and how to file formal charges through the school's grievance procedure or through the legal system depends on several factors. According to Title IX of the 1964 Civil Rights Act, sexual harassment is illegal when it is used as a basis for employment or advancement decisions or creates a hostile environment which interferes with one's work. Beyond these legal definitions, some local policies include the psychological trauma of being a victim of harassment or sexual misconduct.

Upon arriving at a campus, you should immediately get a copy of the school's policy that defines harassment and sexual misconduct and the procedures for filing a grievance. There are significant variations in both definitions and procedures despite the fact that every school that receives federal funds is required to comply with Title IX. Even if you don't need it for yourself, you will most likely be asked for advice and advocacy from female and sometimes male students. You should know the Title IX officer and members of the school's grievance committee.

Whether, when, and how to file a grievance is also a political decision about your own future and goals. Even though these issues have been more widely discussed since Anita Hill made her statement to the U.S. Senate, incidents of harassment and sexual misconduct are not usually efficiently and fairly handled. Instead they trigger reactions that blame the victim and protect perpetrators, especially ones who are well-placed and powerful in the community.

Whenever you become uncomfortable with the comments or behaviors of an administrator, a colleague, a staff member or student and suspect that these incidents are directed at you because of your gender, sexual orientation, ethnicity, physical ability, etc., you should keep a written record giving verbatim accounts of the conversations, their contexts, and specific times and dates. If you don't notice the pattern because of its subtlety until long after it has begun, write down as much as you can remember at the time you become suspicious. Even incidents in which you have some complicity because of your own erotic interests or needs can be considered harassment or misconduct when there is a clear power differential, such as that between Dean and faculty, senior and junior colleagues, and any other difference in rank, gender, sexual orientation, ethnicity or physical ability. What may at first appear to be innocent, welcome, or acceptable behaviors may turn out to be manipulation or coercion after you see the perpetrator's patterns with others. Anyone is vulnerable in certain circumstances, and your own complicity or ignorance does not negate your complaint.

Before you make a complaint, be clear what you want from the process. Remember that you are initiating a formal procedure which will take time and effort, and you need to have the time and resources to make this effort a priority in your life. Committees and procedures are not usually organized to meet the needs of victims, but to adjudicate differences and find the easiest way to solve a problem for the institution. The process can be confusing and you need to set your own agenda.

As soon as you decide that something is wrong that requires action, begin to develop the support base you will need for what will likely be a difficult and dangerous trajectory. Besides keeping careful notes of everything that happens, begin to develop an interpersonal network of people who are sympathetic and can provide emotional support and resources, such as counseling, legal advice, respite, etc. It is often valuable to have an attorney's help as soon as possible. With the help of these persons, develop a written complaint for the grievance procedure or legal action. When you decide to file a complaint, contact the Title IX Officer or other person who is required to hear your complaint and ask for an appointment. This person is usually required to see you within a prescribed time. Take a support person and your written complaint to the meeting. The officer is usually required to hear your complaint without comment or evaluation, but most anything can happen. The training, competence and prejudices of such officers vary enormously, and many see their job as primarily protecting the institution rather than advocating for victims. Don't make any assumptions of benevolence or understanding in your approach. State your complaint simply and clearly and say that you want a full investigation into your charges. You may even say that you have retained a lawyer or obtained legal advice. Legal representation may not be necessary immediately, but it is your right to consult with an attorney before this first meeting. This approach will help to protect you from further harassment and abuse. If your complaint is not accepted by the officer, get a full explanation and afterward write down everything verbatim from the conversation for further appeal. <u>Keeping full notes is necessary at every step of the process.</u>

If your complaint is accepted, there are usually time limits for next steps. For example, the grievance committee may be required to meet within 24-48 hours and receive a copy of your written complaint. You may be required to meet with the committee to restate your complaint. They may be required to send a copy of the complaint to the alleged perpetrator within several days.

Confidentiality is a difficult issue. The Grievance Committee is often required to keep its proceedings secret until a finding has been made. The Committee may also try to elicit or impose an oath of confidentiality on you. You should not give such a promise. Remember that the perpetrator is not bound in any way. He or she may be capable of and willing to destroy your reputation through whatever informal channels are available as a part of the defense. You must be able to act to protect yourself under these conditions, though it is usually better to do so with professional distance rather than out of a wish for personal revenge. Even though you may be justified in your rage and wish for revenge, remember that your goal is to protect yourself and others from such abuse in the future, as well as to be compensated for what has already happened. But the one who harassed or abused you has already shown that he or she has no ethical principles and will likely do whatever is necessary in defense of his or her reputation. Don't mistake any signs of past collegiality from the perpetrator for caring and concern about your welfare.

It is best to decide before you file a complaint what your goals are and how far you want to go. In some cases, the simple act of filing signals your boundaries and serious concern about abusive behaviors. In other cases, you may be committed to taking the process as far as necessary to get an apology and a discussion of the issues within your department or institution. Education of the community is a legitimate reason for filing a complaint, especially if the case you present is a strong one. To stop a perpetrator who has proven to be exceedingly dangerous, you may be determined to take your grievance through the criminal and civil court process. Whatever course you take, you need to count the cost and be willing to persevere until you reach your goals. The backlash against persons who exercise their rights to stop and prevent harassment and sexual misconduct is often severe.

Sometimes the precipitating incident is so traumatic that you will need to act quickly. Events such as rape or a sudden recognition that you have been entrapped in a destructive web of events can interfere with your usual defenses and ways of coping. When the system works, resources such as counseling centers, women's health clinics, and grievance committees should respond to your trauma. Many grievance procedures require the designation of an advocate to help the victim gather her resources and decide what to do. If the system does not work, you should go outside the institution to seek help from advocacy groups such as rape crisis centers or other feminist-oriented crisis programs. These resources will provide the immediate support you need to regroup and decide on your options. You should not be bashful about using the institutional resources to their full extent. But you also need to know that many of these systems remain patriarchal, homophobic and racist, just like the institutions of which they are a part.

The purpose of most grievance procedures is like that of the legal system, namely, to determine the guilt or innocence of the one charged and to recommend appropriate penalties. They have no responsibility to compensate the victim for damages. Any action in that direction must come through negotiation directly with the administration or through civil suit. The grievance committee may, after its investigation, find that no abuse or harassment has occurred and recommend no penalty. Usually such findings are confidential, though a statement to the community may be made if the case has become a public matter. If the grievance committee finds that abuse or harassment has occurred, it can recommend anything from a reprimand to counseling to probation to dismissal. Such judgments usually include a recommendation for action to the president where they can be challenged on the basis of process or outcome. In case you decide to file a civil suit you need to keep careful notes of all events, conversations, and written communication.

For a civil suit you should choose a lawyer carefully. You will need someone who is sympathetic to victims of harassment and sexual misconduct and someone who has special training and experience in this area of the law. Check with feminist groups in the area to find out who is trustworthy. If you are in a rural or isolated area where such resources are not available, ask other female faculty for help or search in the nearest city for a feminist group. Some organizations, such as NOW, the ACLU, and the AAUP have national networks through which you may be able to receive help.

<u>Summary</u>:
1. You should immediately get a copy of the school's policy that defines harassment and sexual misconduct and the procedures for filing a grievance. You should know the Title IX officer and members of the school's grievance committee.
2. As you develop a complaint, set your goals and organize the support base you will need for what will likely be a difficult and dangerous trajectory. Get competent legal advice.
3. Keep full notes every step of the process to protect yourself.
4. Do not give an oath of confidentiality or secrecy and do not trust the process to be benevolent.
5. If the system does not work, you should go outside the institution to seek help from advocacy groups such as rape crisis centers or other feminist-oriented crisis programs.
6. Be prepared to give advice and support to other women who experience harassment or are victims of sexual misconduct.

C.   Helping Others Face Harassment

Because you are a woman, a person of color, and/or a lesbian, women colleagues, staff, and students may bring their initial complaints of harassment to you. You may have to make decisions about advice and advocacy for others. One of the most important changes in recent years is that women are talking about harassment and sexual misconduct with one another. Building this network of conversation and evaluation may be an important part of your teaching and research, as well as your activism for institutional and social change.

When do you encourage and advise someone to make a complaint through the harassment and sexual misconduct grievance procedure? Most procedures can be initiated only by a complaint from the person(s) directly affected. Even abuse that is publicly acknowledged is often excluded from action without a complainant. This means that the decision of the person is primary. Her or his needs should come first. Because over half of all women have been victims of sexual abuse and nearly every woman has experienced sexual harassment, any particular incident can trigger cumulative trauma. For some, proceeding with a complaint can be therapeutic, and the resulting anger can be empowering. Filing a complaint, filing a suit or calling the police can each be appropriate actions in different situations. For other situations, the additional trauma of filing a complaint too soon could jeopardize the person's healing process. (Of course, in cases of rape and/or child sexual abuse, you may be under a moral or legal obligation to file a report of your own). In such cases, providing support and securing medical and counseling services could be the first priority. You should investigate, however, whether there is a statute of limitations on complaints. Limits of six months to two years are not unusual.

You should be aware of your own limits in offering assistance. If you have no training in counseling, it might be wise to refer, gently, a student or colleague who asks you for help to the Counseling center at your institution, to an ombudsperson, or to another person better trained to advocate in such cases. You need not withdraw your support, but knowing how and when you can help will expedite the process.

Most incidents of harassment and sexual misconduct continue to be handled through informal channels within the women's community. At many institutions, a grapevine exists among women (and some men) faculty about which professors sexually harass students. While students are often reluctant to file formal complaints against faculty members, they will sometimes share their experiences with their advisors or other faculty or staff whom they trust. This grapevine provides you with important information for protecting students you advise.

You do not have to state the nature of complaints against a particular professor to steer a student away from that professor's section of a course. If an alternative section is not available, you may encourage a student to seek your help if any problems with that professor arise.

What is at stake is not just developing informal and formal channels to protect women of color, lesbians and others from abuse, but also changing the ethos that keeps such behaviors so numerous, destructive, and invisible. The same political strategies that we use to create secure positions for women must also be used to protect women from abuse and harassment.

RESOURCES

Ellen Bravo and Ellen Cassedy, The 9 to 5 Guide to Combating Sexual Harassment, National Association of Working Women, Wiley, 1992.

Coverdale Sumrall Amber and Dena Taylor, editors, Sexual Harassment: Women Speak Out, introductions by Andrea Dworkin and Margaret Randall, The Crossing Press, 1992.

II. Amorous Relationships With Students

Admission into the ranks of professionals in higher education does not guarantee a woman freedom from sexual harassment, which is why it is important to understand formal and informal strategies for coping with instances when they arise. At the same time, being a professor carries with it responsibilities and a code of professional ethics that pertain to relationships with students, relationships which ought to be characterized by trust and respect. Professors who abuse or appear to abuse trust and respect undermine the faculty-student relationships necessary for effective education. Hence, it is extremely unwise to enter into amorous relationships with students.

Regardless of any feminist or womanist anti-hierarchical sensibilities we may possess, professors in the current world of higher education exercise considerable power over students. We are expected to give praise and criticism, to evaluate and recommend students for future positions and further study, and to participate in conferring awards and benefits on them. Amorous relationships between faculty and students are wrong when a professor has professional responsibility for the student, i.e. any student whose course of study may be impacted by that professor's authority. Such situations greatly increase the chances that a professor may abuse her power over the student, that evaluation of the student by other faculty and students may be affected by suspicions of favoritism in the professor involved, and that the professor may face charges of sexual harassment or exploitation, should the relationship sour. Amorous relationships often place faculty in positions of serious conflicts of interest. Other faculty may begin to avoid a colleague because of their discomfort with an amorous relationship.

Even when amorous relationships are consensual, they may not appear so if the student or professor seems to gain from such a relationship. When power inequities are structured into a relationship from the beginning (as they are in higher education) and the student is young, there are questions about what mutual consent means when the parties involved are not equal in power. Even when a student initiates such a relationship and pursues it aggressively, you should, as a professional, discourage any such intent. A student may pursue an amorous relationship with a professor that compromises the professor, for example, to improve grades, to receive a good recommendation, to gain access to other professionals in the same field, or to repeat past self-destructive behaviors. A student may be a victim of incest and have learned to behave seductively toward parental authority figures. Students can be very appealing and persistent, and resisting succumbing to such advances requires a clear sense of professional ethics, self-possession, and knowledge of one's own psychological weaknesses. Cultivate these attributes--they will serve you well throughout your career. Maintaining professional relationships benefits both you and students. Such professional relationships can often be warm and develop into fine friendships, but to the extent a student gains a lover, she or he loses a teacher, mentor, model and guide.

If, as occasionally happens in close working relationships, you find yourself in a relationship with a student that is moving toward deeper involvement, it is wise to postpone changing the relationship until the student can no longer be affected by your authority, either because she or he graduates or transfers. A professional reputation, known for its fairness, integrity, and adherence to ethical principles, can be lost forever by one untimely involvement with a student. Faculty have been known to lose their jobs because of such affairs, and even if you stay at an institution, you may find yourself shut out of leadership opportunities and alienated from your colleagues. Weigh the consequences of your decision carefully before pursuing an amorous relationship with a student. Facing the consequences may be much more difficult than creating your social life off campus.

CONCLUSION: EMPOWERING WOMEN
IN RELIGIOUS STUDIES

"Sisterhood is powerfu!" is the way many white, middle class women described the phenomenon of the modern women's movement in the seventies. "Networking" is the phrase that replaced sisterhood in the eighties (evoking the materialism of that decade). In the nineties, as women in academic religion, we are more diverse in race, ethnicity, class, and national origins, and we seek to be both less personalistic (sisterhood) and less dominated by values of the middle class (networking). We seek in this survival manual to be differently political because we work in academic institutions enmeshed in patriarchal systems and within which we believe it is possible to organize strategically for change and women's empowerment. We hope to convey a sense of pragmatism: it is wise neither to despair of these systems nor to trust them to be benign. If we were to design a slogan for the nineties, it might be 'analyze together, organize, and survive.'

The work of analysis and its role in women's survival in the field of academic religion is part of the charge given to the Committee on the Status of Women in the Profession when it was brought into being in 1990. The charge states, "The Committee on the Status of Women in the Profession shall study the problems of women in religious studies, propose remedies and initiatives that can be undertaken by offices of the Academy, receive and review communications and recommendations on the topic from the membership, and develop ways to involve men as well as women in addressing these issues."

During its first year, as the committee listened to its membership in the American Academy of Religion, as well as members of the Society of

Biblical Literature, the American Historical Association and the Modern Languages Association, it became clear that one useful "remedy" was a guide for women negotiating work in the field. Both the AHA and the MLA have such guides and they have been successful. This manual was developed in response to the many communications and recommendations we have had from the membership to "do something about sexual harassment." (The chapter in the manual is only one of the strategies we have undertaken with regard to this difficult issue.) In addition, the manual addresses many more concerns of women seeking careers in religious studies.

We expect this manual to be useful to men as well as women, particularly to administrators who find themselves negotiating with women scholars over the very issues we raise. We also feel that in the absence of a similar mentoring process for younger men in the academy, the manual could simply be of practical help to a younger male scholar who has to traverse some, if not all, of the same turbulent waters of finding a job, negotiating an offer, getting tenure, publishing, etc. The manual can be of particular help to men who face discrimination according to race, ethnicity, or sexual preference.

The editors of the manual expect that it will be revised and re-printed after this first edition. I too have that expectation. I want to echo their request for suggestions for changes and additions.

We actually had quite a bit of fun putting this manual together: sharing war stories, laughing over clever responses to difficult questions, proposing unprintable advice. We also mourned over stories of those who have not been able to negotiate the many difficulties women face in this field. We hope that you too, as a member of our field, will celebrate our victories, mourn our defeats, and be with us in the struggle. As was said during a different political movement: if we don't hang together, we all hang separately.

Dr. Susan Brooks Thistlethwaite
Chairperson, The Committee on the Status of Women in the Profession of the American Academy of Religion